Woman's
Wales?

Dr Emma Schofield is a writer, academic and essayist with a specialism in the intersection between politics and culture in Wales. She is Editor of *Wales Arts Review* and has published widely on a range of topics relating to Wales, devolution, literature and women in politics. She is also a regular contributor to a range of radio and television programmes, including Radio 4's *Front Row*, the Arts Show on BBC Radio Wales and *Politics Wales* on BBC One Wales. Emma's PhD thesis explored the connection between literature and devolution in Wales and she has written widely in the representation of women in culture and politics in Wales. In addition to her work as a writer and editor, Emma teaches at Cardiff University, where she specialises in education development.

Woman's Wales?

The Dissonance and Diversity of Devolution through the lives of Women in Wales

Edited by

Emma Schofield

PARTHIAN

Parthian, Cardigan SA43 1ED
www.parthianbooks.com
© all contributors 2024
ISBN 978-1-914595-47-9
Editor: Emma Schofield
Typeset by Elaine Sharples
Cover designer: Emily Courdelle
Printed by 4edge Limited
Published with the support of the Books Council of Wales
British Library Cataloguing in Publication Data.
A cataloguing record for this book is available from the British Library.
Every attempt has been made to secure the permission of copyright
holders to reproduce archival and printed material.
Printed on FSC accredited paper.

For Chloe and Isabel

CONTENTS

DEVOLUTION AND DAUGHTERS: BUILDING POLITICAL MOMENTUM ACROSS GENERATIONS

By Emma Schofield

I've often wondered whether, as a writer and editor, I'm talking about women too much; it certainly seems to be the topic I spend the most time writing about these days. When that thought pops into my mind, usually while my coffee is going cold as I try to juggle finishing a piece of work with getting my daughters ready for school, I remind myself of exactly why it's so important that we do keep talking about women in Wales. Writing for *Wales Arts Review* back in 2018 I argued that equality in Wales was in everyone's interests and here I am, over five years later, about to make the same argument again, but with an even greater sense of urgency.

In reality, that same argument is still so important and the case for true equality for women in Wales still needs making. Looking back at that article, it's hard not to feel as if progress along that rocky path has not so much faltered as ground to a halt. Something in 2018 felt different; the vision set out by the Welsh Government in a speech by then First Minister, Carwyn Jones, was full of hope and purpose, predicated on the principle that 'a gender-equal Wales means an equal sharing of power, resources and influence for all women, men and non-binary people.' Jones went on to assert that 'this is a vision

1

where the government aims to create the conditions for equality of outcome for all'. Five years after this decision, and well into another term of Welsh Government, and there clearly remains much work to be done to achieve this goal, not only to ensure gender parity within government structures in Wales, but to establish an environment in which political decisions are made that not only strive for equality, but seek to genuinely improve the lives of the next generation of women in Wales.

Perhaps using the term 'next generation' seems somewhat defeatist. After all, a good starting point for improving the lives of women in Wales would arguably be to better the lives of all women living in Wales, right now. The trouble is, that's much easier said than done. The essays in this collection beautifully, and lyrically, exemplify the challenges and struggles of being a woman in Wales. They touch on topics such as education, healthcare and maternity, disability, the arts, politics and sexuality; they are diverse in their approach and in their tone, oscillating between moments of joy and moments of real frustration. They are made up of stories of experience and reflection on what devolution has really meant for women, a quarter of a century after the official opening of the first Welsh Assembly. Their voices are individual, yet they are bound together by one common theme: a desire to focus not on the events of the past, but on how these events might be used to shape a better, stronger, future for women as Wales moves forward into this next era of devolution. If we are to secure genuine change for the next generation, we need to hear all of these voices.

To make progress, we must acknowledge what has been both good and bad about the trajectory of women's lives in Wales since the introduction of devolution.

Which is, broadly speaking, how this collection came about. The idea for the book was born out of conversations which occurred not in academic conferences, or research forums and institutes, but in person, in coffee shops or supermarkets, or online through email exchanges. Each piece was initially born out of a discussion about what being a woman in Wales really means after twenty-five years of devolution and how we'd like the future to look. Discussing the project with some of the contributors, I asked them not to focus on celebrating or criticising devolution, but on evaluating an aspect of how it had affected their own lives. Above all else I asked them to be honest, to chart their own journey, as women, through one element of their lives under a devolved government in Wales; to focus not on lamenting the past, but on recognising how that past might better inform the coming years.

Thinking about how I first became interested in our political identity in Wales, I realise that my own journey with devolution began a long time ago. I was in school at the time that Wales went to the polls for a second referendum on devolution in 1997, having roundly rejected the concept almost twenty years earlier in the referendum of 1979. That shadow of 1979 was never far away from the debate which unfolded in the lead up to the 1997 referendum. One of my strongest memories of that time is of my own mother, leaning out of a car window to wave to campaigners lining the streets of Cardiff who were out in an attempt to drum up support for a devolved administration a few days ahead of the vote. Perhaps that's how my own conversations about devolution began, through talking to my mother, asking questions and wanting to understand exactly why she was so keen to see the prospect of a Welsh Assembly brought to life. At the time, I was too young to understand the full political ramifications of the decision the country was facing, but I remember my mum's enthusiasm for the *potential* of what that decision might offer us.

Over a quarter of a century later, I am able to revisit the threads of that conversation with my mum, only to find a very different tone had replaced the enthusiasm and hope I'd remembered so vividly from 1997. I begin by asking her what being a student in the build-up to the 1979 referendum on devolution had meant to her perception of devolution. 'As an active member of the Student's Union at Swansea University, I supported the idea of devolution for Wales', she tells me, recalling her work on the 'Yes' campaign, alongside fellow students. 'We were part of the Broad Left, opposed to the conservatives and also to extreme left-wing groups. The government in Westminster felt stale and the idea of a Welsh Assembly seemed to offer the hope of a new way, a fresh way of doing things and a chance to elect politicians who would work exclusively in the interests of ordinary Welsh people.' She tells me that there was a sense of weariness in the air at the time, a frustration that 'we were always just an afterthought in any decisions taken

4

by the Westminster government. In 1979 we thought devolution would give recognition to the fact that although we are part of the Unted Kingdom, Wales has an identity of its own; our problems and economic needs were not necessarily the same as those in many parts of England.'

Her account of a sense of hope, mired in a frustration at the inability to move forward, is mirrored by the wider cultural mood at the time. While a small but determined section of voters fought fiercely for what it believed was the only way to secure a much-needed degree of autonomy for 1970s' Wales, there remained a significant degree of opposition to the notion of devolution. It was a struggle which was fiercely entangled in a far-reaching struggle to re-align the country's political history with the hope of what it might achieve in a more autonomous future. Jane Aaron notes this tension in her piece on the development of Welsh fiction in the post-1979 era, noting that there was a pull towards devolution from some quarters, pitted against a Wales which had shown campaigners 'good reason to fear that contemporary Wales was more afraid of freedom than death itself'.[1]

Reflecting on this sense of determined optimism among 'Yes' campaigners in 1979, I ask my mum what she felt the driving force was behind the campaign within her own student body:

'We were idealistic and we believed that devolution offered hope for a better future, a more modern way of

---

[1] Jane Aaron, 'Towards Devolution: New Welsh Writing', in *The Cambridge History of Twentieth-Century English Literature*, ed. Laura Marcus and Peter Nicholls (Cambridge: Cambridge University Press, 2004), pp. 685-699, p. 688.

doing things so that the needs of Wales could be prioritised. As the referendum, drew closer it became clear to us that many people in Wales did not support devolution. Handing out leaflets in Swansea's newly opened quadrant centre, most people were simply not interested in the campaign. More vociferous men simply asked, "Why don't you just go home, love?" and by the weekend before the referendum we were deflated. We realised that the vote would most likely be a "No" and although the result wasn't a shock, it did leave us disillusioned. It felt as if people were rejecting change and the opportunity for more of a say in our future; it was depressing and, as a female, it seemed demoralising that power would remain where it had always been, firmly in the hands of the male majority in Westminster.'

It is that sense of frustration over power remaining so tantalisingly close, and yet so firmly beyond reach, which underscores discussions about how devolution came into existence in Wales. The introduction of devolution in Wales was not a rapid one; indeed, the vote in favour of devolution for Wales marked only the start of a lengthy process to restructure Welsh political power.

Delivering a lecture in 1998, Labour Assembly Member Ron Davies famously commented that devolution was 'a process and not an event' and that 'its impact will be on the whole of our public, economic, social and political life'.[2] The National Assembly was not

---

[2] Ron Davies 'Devolution: a process not an event', Reardon-Smith lecture theatre, National Museum of Wales, Cardiff (February 4th, 1999).

officially opened in Wales until 1999, with the first Assembly Members being elected during May of the same year. Even the decision on where to house the new National Assembly had not proved easy, causing a considerable amount of speculation and disagreement between political parties and the public. Plans were unveiled for a brand-new assembly building which would be built in Cardiff Bay at the cost of approximately twenty-seven million pounds, while a rival bid suggested housing the assembly in Swansea's Guildhall. Several arguments were raised against the option to build a new assembly building in the Bay, not least the fact that as a region Cardiff had voted against devolution in both the 1979 and 1997 referenda. The decision proved so controversial that a special report by the BBC in 1998 branded the process a 'bad advertisement for the ability of Wales to run its own affairs'.[3] Resolution was eventually reached when Assembly Members voted in favour of the proposals for a new building in Cardiff Bay, although it would take until 2006 for the new Senedd building to be completed and officially opened. While logistical decisions about the building and the purpose, and responsibility, of the new National Assembly for Wales characterised those early years of devolution, the question of what this seismic political change would mean for women remained largely unexplored.

Without doubt, devolution in Wales has afforded the

---

[3] Glyn Matthias, 'What Next for Wales?', a BBC Special Report. January 1, 1998. http://news.bbc.co.uk/1/hi/special_report/for_christmas/_new_year/devolutio n/39994.stm [Accessed 26/04/2013].

opportunity for the redefinition of place and identity to some extent. Writing in 2007, Katie Gramich argued that 'The "Yes" vote in the Devolution Referendum of 1997 and the subsequent creation of the Welsh Assembly have undoubtedly changed both the concept and the reality of "Wales" as a political and, arguably, a cultural and social place'.[4] For Gramich, the emergence of this new sense of place is a defining factor in the resurgence of Welsh female writers during the twenty-first century. It certainly felt, for a while, as if there was some momentum behind the move for a brighter and more equitable society in the wake of devolution, but that promise does not appear to have come fully to fruition. In this collection, in Jasmine Donahaye's analysis of the visibility of female figures within contemporary Welsh culture, she asserts that 'looking back, it's clear how in that post-devolution moment of cultural expansion, old familiar patterns were being reinforced in new ways'; a sobering reminder that the excitement of devolution did not automatically equate to increased cultural prominence for women in Wales.

Of course, it hasn't all been doom and gloom. When it comes to the cultural landscape Wales has always boasted a strong female voice; there is a lengthy canon of Welsh women writers, musicians and artists, and even though they have not always achieved the recognition they so richly deserve, they have often flourished, albeit against the odds. In politics, however, the picture has always looked somewhat different. Wales' first female MP came

---

[4] Katie Gramich, *Twentieth-Century Welsh Women's Writing: Land, Gender, Belonging* (Cardiff: University of Wales Press, 2007), p. 183.

in 1929 when Lady Megan Lloyd George was elected as the representative for Anglesey for the Liberal party, going on to become a key campaigner for Welsh Government and a strong advocate for the introduction of a Secretary of State for Wales. Ironically, although the role of Secretary of State was eventually introduced in 1964, it is a post which has only once, in over half a century, been held by a female MP. Conservative MP Cheryl Gillan held the role for just two years, from 2010 – 2012, before being replaced, against her wishes, during a cabinet reshuffle.

For a short while it seemed as if devolution may have brought the dawn of a new era to politics in Wales. There was, in 2003, a brief moment of utopia when the National Assembly comprised an equal number of elected male and female Assembly Members, making it the first legislature in the world to achieve a gender balance among its elected members. Indeed, there was even a year when, following a by-election in 2006, the gender balance in the National Assembly tipped in favour of women, with no less than thirty-one of the sixty seats being held by women. Yet a closer look at these figures reveals a more complex situation. It is broadly acknowledged that the gender balance in the Assembly was achieved through the somewhat controversial use of all-women shortlists and a complex 'twinning' system designed to enforce equal representation across neighbouring constituencies, particularly within the Labour party. It is also worth noting that in spite of this milestone, many of the most senior roles within the Assembly still eluded female

Members. In 2006, for example, many of the highest-ranking roles, including those of First Minister, Minister for Health and Social Services, Presiding Officer and Deputy Presiding Officer, were all held by male Assembly Members. Notwithstanding the lack of women in senior ministerial roles, it is easy to underestimate the magnitude of this achievement; an outcome which positioned Wales as a leader in gender parity in politics on an international platform. Unfortunately, the promise and excitement held in this brief moment of parity did not last long.

By the time of the Welsh Assembly election in 2007, a mere four years on, the numbers had shifted and the equality balance which had marked Wales out as a world-leader for gender equality in politics, was no longer there. While the numbers of female Assembly Members initially remained encouraging, those numbers have declined over the proceeding years; following the results of the last Senedd elections in May 2021 women held just 43% of seats in the Senedd Chamber. Although this figure is still a higher proportion than the equivalent statistic in the Westminster government, which currently sits at 34%, it is still some way off the lofty heights achieved by the second Senedd. Moreover, a closer look at the representation of women in local councils across Wales shows that, in the Autumn of 2021, just six of Wales' twenty-two councils had a female leader, while only four of those councils boasted a gender-equal cabinet. Unsurprisingly, the reasons for this lack of women at both a national and local level are not straightforward. Pressures with regard to childcare and family responsibility have long acted as a barrier to women in politics, as has the struggle to enter a sphere which has, traditionally, been a predominantly male space. Such issues are not exclusive to national levels, but also exist within local government. Testimonies given to the Expert Group on Diversity in Local Government, for a report in 2013, highlighted similar issues, including the difficulty of standing as a female councillor in areas historically dominated by male representatives. In the report, county councillor Karen Elizabeth Pearson described how there are 'many barriers faced by rural women, particularly within politics, as this has been the Bastille of men for many years and as a result women are not always taken seriously or given the opportunities afforded to men.' Over a decade on from this report, it is clear that the measures suggested by the Group, which included cross-party strategies to widen participation, have not worked as hoped.

In spite of no longer holding the mantle of a gender-equal legislature, it's important to note that there are still a number of positive signs within the gender balance in the Senedd. Since the birth of Welsh devolution, the proportion of elected female representatives has remained one of the highest percentages in the world when compared to other, similar legislative bodies. As noted above, there has been some considerable fluctuation at each fresh set of elections; yet in spite of this fluctuation, twenty-six out of sixty seats in the Senedd are currently held by women. This is, however, only one facet of the complicated task of establishing a feminist government for Wales. Working to promote and maintain this balance is important and having an equal government for Wales is, without doubt, something to strive for, but what matters most are the decisions which are being made at ground level and the proportion of female representation of government in Wales. Laura McAllister, Professor at the Wales Governance Centre at Cardiff University, blogged in 2018 about the fact that 'in Wales – like virtually everywhere else – around 80% of all powerful, decision-making roles are held by men' and this fact continues to be an indisputable obstacle on the course towards gender equality.[5] As McAllister points out, this figure has to change if these roles are to become genuinely representative of the women who make up 52% of our population in Wales. When it comes to leadership roles within Welsh politics and governance, women are still far too notable by their absence.

None of which is to say that nothing positive has happened as a result of the devolution referendum. There have been a number of actions taken at a local government level which have made strides towards improving the lives of women in Wales. The challenge is that making a real change means committing to support women in every phase of their lives, which requires a broader national steer. For example, back in 2018, Rhondda Cynon Taff voted to become one of the first councils in Wales to provide free sanitary products to all schoolgirls. The vote was a massive step forward in the

---

[5] Laura McAllister, 'The Basic Truth About Men, Women and Power in Wales', *Wales Online*, 17th March, 2018.

fight to end so called 'period poverty' in Wales, and yet the very fact that in 2018 such a problem still existed is astounding. We cannot consider ourselves to be a fully civilised and compassionate nation while we still have girls suffering the indignity of struggling through their monthly menstrual cycle without access to sanitary products, in some cases also missing out on valuable days of their education as a result.

The decision of the council in Rhondda Cynon Taff was a bold one and went on to pave the way for similar decisions across all councils in Wales. Following the decision made by the council in Rhondda Cynon Taff, the Welsh Government announced an investment of one million pounds to help tackle period poverty, aimed at providing access to sanitary products to girls and young women in communities where period poverty is at its highest. Yet this kind of investment must be maintained in order to create a lasting value and instil a legacy of change. If we really want to push for progress for women in Wales then that progress has to cover all areas of women's lives and not ignore the problems which may be difficult for men to talk about, or those which make for uncomfortable conversations. It is these difficulties that the pieces in this collection explore, and such conversations which they seek to instigate.

Indeed, the contributions in this collection are packed with examples of how women's lives are still being enormously affected by the pressures of childcare, caring responsibilities and outdated attitudes, both within and outside of, politics. We start with Mari Ellis Dunning's powerful account of the mental and physical impact of a healthcare system which is struggling to provide adequate support for women, particularly in the spheres of gynaecological and perinatal care, drawn in part from her own experiences. Similar concerns rear their head in a number of the pieces, not least in a very timely assessment of maternal care and responsibilities, by Nansi Eccott and Jessica Laimann, based on research from the Women's Equality Network Wales. In both pieces, the question of how female voices are represented and heard within our healthcare system, is paramount. Such discussion is also addressed through Yvonne Murphy's reflections on future for cultural industries in Wales, which asks what kind of society we want in order to facilitate the sharing of narratives and the growth of ideas.

That issue of voices, and the ways in which they are heard, is also central in Krystal S. Lowe's reflection on her own identity as a Black woman and a freelance practitioner within the creative industries in Wales. Connecting her freelance career with her identity as a mother to her young child, Lowe's poetic response 'What Am I Building?' poses a poignant question:

'What am I building? What will I leave behind for Young Lowe, for the world?

For Young Lowe, I hope to leave him with the courage to be his full self, to be empowered in who he is and what he is passionate about and to love the world enough to seek empowerment for others.

For Wales, I hope to see a generation of empowered,

confident, connected Black women who courageously innovate their work and bring others along with them. I hope to rebalance inequity, teach others the importance of and skill to integrate access in all of their work.'

Lowe's focus on the future and the building of a society in which all women are empowered, confident and connected, sets out a vision for a Wales where women have the ability to balance all elements of their professional, personal and family lives, without restriction or limitation.

Building on this focus, Lowe's chapter also returns us to the concept of motherhood as a driving force for change in the lives of women in Wales, one which echoes throughout a number of the other pieces within this collection. Motherhood lies at the heart of Sophie Buchaillard's reflections on migrancy and its problematic implications in terms of our historical and cultural identities, as well as finding its way into Rae Howells' evocative exploration of devolution and climate change in Wales. Everywhere we turn, those generational bonds can be found, driving forward the desire for a Wales which is truly progressive and which offers a commitment to creating a fairer and more sustainable future. Likewise, the significance of reconciliation – between historical attitudes and progressive policy when it comes to female sexuality – lies at the heart of Norena Shopland's discussion of the Welsh Government's remarkable change of direction in its LGBTQ+ Action Plan. Here, Shopland sets out how the Welsh Government has been able to lead the way in the development of such a plan, in part by encouraging the celebration of local voices and providing a platform for individual stories to be heard.

Drawing these different pieces together has been emotionally complex. On one hand, there is that hope that a more equitable, and much kinder, society lies ahead of us within Wales. On the other, there is a sense of uncertainty about how we can move forward from the vague notion of 'feminist government' which was set out in 2018, coupled with disappointment that the hope and potential of those early years of devolution has not been fully realised. I finish the conversation with my mum by asking how she feels, looking back at these first twenty-five years of devolution in Wales.

'I would definitely say that I am disillusioned. When the "Yes" campaign won through in 1997, albeit by a small majority, I was delighted. It seemed that my hopes for the future, which had been dashed in 1979, would now be fulfilled. I don't feel that way now. I believe that the opportunities have been wasted and money has been squandered. The Welsh Government itself often seems undemocratic and does not want to listen to the people it was elected to represent and work for. I am disillusioned and feel disenfranchised; the Labour Party, which has held power in Wales throughout the twenty-five years of devolution, has failed to improve the standards in key areas of Welsh life and there seem to be no viable alternatives among the other parties. I question whether I would campaign or vote for devolution today, based on what we have experienced since 1997.'

It is difficult to reconcile this sense of deflation with the excitement and hope I remember being so prevalent in my memories of the 1997 referendum. And yet, I know that there is growing dissatisfaction around the progress made by a Welsh Government whose ambitions often seem to outstrip its own ability to deliver on the concepts it so painstakingly outlines. That same sense of disenfranchisement may account, in part, for the results of a 2020 poll carried out by YouGov and ITV, which found that 22% of respondents wanted no devolution in Wales, and that 25% were in favour of abolition of the Senedd, with 48% opposed to abolition.[6] The numbers point, overwhelmingly, to the likelihood of a continuation of Wales' turbulent relationship with devolution. Debate over whether Wales should ultimately seek full political independence, would appear to have done little to assuage this sense of uncertainty about the country's political future.

As I write this piece, towards the end of 2023, things feel more than a little bleak. Headlines about women in Wales this year have been dominated by stories which seem to paint an alarming picture about the state of women's lives across the nation. In September, research taken from a survey by the Open University found that, in Wales, almost a fifth of women have experienced online

---

[6] Poll quoted in Awan-Scully, Roger (5 June, 2020). 'With Welsh independence polling higher than ever it is no longer a fringe movement', *Nation Cymru*.

violence; notably more than the fifteen percent of women in England and the approximately twelve percent in Northern Ireland.[7] This news was followed later in the Autumn by a report from FOR Cardiff, a group representing businesses in the city, which found that one in five women respondents reported that they did not venture out after dark because of concerns about safety. Meanwhile the implementation of the much-awaited 'Women and Girls Health Plan' has so far been mired by delays and uncertainty surrounding the next steps. The bigger picture feels far from hopeful and the prospect of real change to the circumstances faced by women across the country still seems to be agonisingly out of reach.

What is, perhaps, most frustrating about this situation in which we find ourselves in 2023, is that it is not entirely unexpected. A 2010 review by The Hansard Society, commissioned by the British Council Scotland, entitled 'Has Devolution Delivered for Women?', explored the impact of devolution on the lives of women in Scotland and Wales a decade into devolution. The report concluded that 'the battle for women's equal representation in Edinburgh and Cardiff was far from won, and that urgent further action was needed to ensure that the progress of the previous decade would be sustained in the next.'[8] In its findings, the report also

---

[7] 'Almost one fifth of women in Wales experience online violence, survey finds', ITV Wales, September 7th 2023. https://www.itv.com/news/wales/2023-09-07/nearly-17-of-women-in-wales-experience-online-violence-survey-finds.

[8] The Hansard Society, 'Has Devolution Delivered for Women?', May 24th 2010. https://www.hansardsociety.org.uk/publications/reports/has-devolution-delivered-for-women.

noted that 'voluntary action by political parties is not enough. The progress it delivers is vulnerable both to change within key parties and to the shifting balance of power between them. There is therefore a case for reopening the debate about whether equal representation of women should be guaranteed by constitutional and electoral law, rather than purely by action within parties'. To date, in spite of this recommendation, no significant progress has been made in respect of this debate, with the number of female representatives within the Welsh Government continuing to decline in recent Senedd elections. The warning signs were there just one decade into devolution in Wales but, to date, the country's ability to adequately respond to those warning signs has appeared considerably limited.

So where does this leave us, a quarter of a century on from a political decision which has, arguably, never lived up to its full potential? In 2017, twenty years after that second devolution referendum, I became a mother to my own daughter, followed in 2020 by the birth of my second daughter, during the Covid-19 pandemic. On a personal level, the transition to becoming a mum to two young girls has prompted a renewed sense of concern about the position of women within our arts, cultural and political spheres. More broadly, I want my children to grow to become part of a Wales which offers them a fair and equitable space for their voices, as women, to be heard; in which they will have access to education, politics and healthcare and in which they will be able to develop as individuals and to make their own contribution to society in a way which feels safe and secure. Surely that's not too much to ask? Grace Quantock, in her piece on public life and marginalised bodies in Wales, writes of how decision-making capabilities are not always fairly applied, throwing out the question: 'how are those places earned and who gets to speak and to listen when it comes to our country's healthcare, social care, arts, digital infrastructure and human rights?'. That question, which cuts to the heart of the debate within this collection, must become the glimmer of light which guides our discussion about how best to create a fairer society for women in Wales.

If we are to move forward, making progress towards a more equitable Wales, we must find a way to address that question of who is given a place at the table when it comes to making political and social decisions for our nation. Women need to be included, not in order to fulfil a statutory obligation, or to meet a minimum required number, but because they have an invaluable contribution to make and because their voices must be heard. Turning that hope into a reality is, of course, a much bigger project than exploring these ideas within the pages of a book and yet, these discussions may prove to be a catalyst for a broader debate about the future of devolution in Wales and where women sit within that future. For now, I suspect that I will continue to spend a significant portion of my time, within my writing and as an editor, exploring these questions and encouraging that debate to continue to grow. And that's okay; what we desperately need is not only to keep talking about women in Wales, but to keep reading about them, to keep thinking about their history and their futures and to keep on asking questions about how we can make things better, however difficult those questions may be to answer.

'THE WORDS SHE'S KEPT IN': HEALTHCARE BIAS IN WALES AND BEYOND

By Mari Ellis Dunning

> 'the doctor
> keeps telling her it's nothing as they rise
> like stings, the words she's kept in.'
> — 'Burning Mouth Syndrome'
> by Victoria Gatehouse

Following the implementation of new sexual education guidance across the UK in 2017, the Welsh government used their devolved powers to make 'Relationship and Sexuality Education' compulsory as part of the curriculum in Welsh schools. As a result, as of September 2022, parents no longer have the power to withdraw their children from these lessons. Inevitably, there has been some backlash from parents who believe they should have the right to keep their children from this vital learning, as well as from a small, but active, campaign group,[1] driven mostly by unfounded fears about what their children will be taught.

There are numerous reasons I support the move to make RSE compulsory in Wales: the aim to foster

---

[1] The activist group, Child Protection Wales, have spearheaded a campaign to stop the compulsory RSE bill, handing leaflets to parents at school gates and posting them through the letterboxes of the general public.

inclusivity, equality and diversity through teaching children about the variations in family dynamics; to educate children about consent, boundaries and bodily autonomy; and to ensure sexual health and wellbeing in the next generation amongst them.

Other benefits aside, my focus for the purposes of this essay is the impact that comprehensive sex education in Welsh schools could have on the treatment of women and girls in healthcare settings in Wales for generations to come.

Decent sex education was lacking when I grew up in the nineties and noughties. From what I recall, during the last year of primary school, we were given a brief session about menstruation, delivered by a nurse to the girls in the class only. Then in comprehensive school, there was a handful of sessions delivered by a biology teacher, which involved watching a very dated video about grooming, and dipping a tampon into a cup of water. The majority of students had started their periods by this point, and at least some were already sexually active. Again, boys and girls were separated. It was woefully inadequate.

At present, gender-based bias in healthcare is a huge and ongoing issue. Though we cannot blame the school curriculum and insufficient sex education for centuries of poor understanding of the female body and dangerous medical bias, implementing comprehensive teaching, for both sexes, is certainly a sensible place to begin to tackle these huge societal gaps, which have their grounding as far back as ancient Egypt.

1. Hysteria and the Roaming Womb

'Perhaps you've never had to wear
your own discomfort to keep yourself in check.'
– 'Pineapple (Objects in a Portrait 1)'
by Angela Cleland

The word hysteria (to be frenzied, frantic and out of control) originates from the Greek for uterus – *hystera*. Hysteria is thereby a sex-specific problem, an affliction attributed to only the female population. In ancient Egyptian and Greek societies, behavioural abnormalities in women were often attributed to hysteria, a condition believed at the time to be caused by a roaming, or wandering, womb. Later, it was believed symptoms of hysteria derived from fluid buildup around the uterus, and so the obvious solution and general medical recommendation throughout history was regular sexual intercourse – male semen was also believed to have healing properties. In the 1800s, Freud famously developed his own theories regarding hysteria, suggesting symptoms were caused by psychological damage at the 'Oedipal moment of recognition,' in which a young woman realises she has no penis, placing men as the standardised norm by which others are defined. In short, male figures and medical practitioners throughout history have been obsessed with their phallic organs, viewing women as either in need of penile penetration, or envious at their lack of male genitals. Yes, really.

The cure for women who were unable to receive sexual stimulation (unmarried maidens, widows, nuns) was uterine massage – which is, unfortunately, exactly what it sounds like. Doctors at the time were so concerned with this treatment becoming conflated with sex that some even advocated hurting their patients, or at least causing discomfort. Thankfully, we now know that the uterus is not at the heart of all female medical issues, and that most symptoms historically attributed to hysteria were likely the result of mental illness, stress, postpartum issues, and other undesirable gendered ailments – restlessness, assertiveness, ambition, will, drive. Hysteria, then, was essentially the medical diagnosis for anything society found troubling and unmanageable in a woman. Use of the term abounds today: as recently as 2022, minister Lee Waters referred to a female opponent's comments as 'hysterical'.

Although hysteria was only removed from the Official Diagnostic and Statistical Manual of Mental Disorders as recently as 1980, the world of medicine has changed considerably, with much better understanding and documentation of women's anatomy (although a quick scan of Reddit's 'Bad Women's Anatomy' proves how much education is lacking in this area. If you're yet to discover this subreddit, I suggest you grab a glass of gin and clear your schedule). Regardless, misdiagnosis, through varied combinations of dismissal of women's pain, ignorance, arrogance and bias, remains rife.

Where this gap really opens into a chasm is in areas of healthcare specifically centred around women: contraceptive services and family planning; maternity services; postnatal support, in particular lactation; and generally anything to do with the female reproductive system. An off the cuff example: despite affecting one in ten women in the UK, following the first consultation with a GP, it takes an average of eight or nine years to be diagnosed with endometriosis, a painful and often debilitating condition in which tissue similar to the lining of the womb grows in other places, doubling a woman's chances of infertility.

Both anecdotes and academic research point to a disturbing tendency within the medical industry to dismiss women's pain. One study found that women visiting emergency departments with 'acute pain' were less likely than men to be prescribed opioids and to subsequently wait longer to receive them. Women's pain is also much more likely to be dismissed as 'anxiety', and women are far more likely to be written off as psychiatric patients even when their ailments are physical. This pain bias taps into wider biases amongst physicians and other medical professionals that have been uncovered in recent years, with one study showing that patients with more feminine personality traits across both sexes and genders had a higher risk of poor access to care.

These issues affect women across the home nations, with no immediately apparent difference in management or outcomes for patients in Wales compared with other parts of the UK, nor other European countries. In fact, across Europe, women are more frequently diagnosed with 'depression' and men with 'stress', based on the same complaints. But what if we could use our powers as a devolved country to strengthen women's medical experiences? In researching this essay, I uncovered endless accounts of experiences of inadequate healthcare in Wales, ranging from inconvenient to life-changing and even fatal. I'll begin with my own...

Following an issue with cervical bleeding, it took over five years, countless GP consultations, and repeated STI screening, for me to finally be diagnosed with a cervical ectropion. The issue wasn't that an ectropion is difficult to detect, but rather that each practitioner I saw would simply send me for an STI test and dismiss me, with no follow up when the test proved negative (as I invariably assured them it would). Given my age at the time, I can understand why STIs were the first consideration for the countless doctors I consulted, but all it took was for one practitioner to actually listen to me: to trust what I was saying about my sexual history; to trust what I was telling them about my partner's sexual history; to trust me when I told them I had already been tested for STIs, numerous times. I was lucky – a cervical ectropion is inconvenient and messy at best, and frightening at worst. It's not serious or life-threatening. But what if it had been?

This brings me to a much more troubling story. During my second year at university, my housemate and close friend was diagnosed with Stage 4 Leukaemia. It took her four or five trips to the GP before she was taken seriously and referred for blood tests, when her initial diagnosis of tonsillitis failed to improve. Shockingly, paracetamol does not cure cancer. Thinking about women who are not taken seriously: there was the friend who was prescribed a higher dose of antidepressants when the real issue was domestic abuse, another friend whose coeliac disease was attributed to depression, the neighbour whose spinal problem was blamed on postnatal depression, and the acquaintance whose appendicitis was misdiagnosed as anxiety. I can't help but think of the countless women I know who have been offered nothing but paracetamol for their pain following a caesarean section (a massive and invasive operation), despite guidelines recommending opioids as standard.

Gendered stereotypes have caused tremendous damage throughout history, and, as evidenced in the cases already detailed, continue to do so. In fact, compared with men, women with ACS (better known as a heart attack) have higher odds of presenting with pain between the shoulder blades, nausea, vomiting and shortness of breath, and lower odds of presenting with the more typically recognised chest pain. The presence of sex differences in symptom presentation has been established since the early 2000s, but anecdotally tends to be virtually unheard of. This can be attributed in part to a baseline dismissal of women's pain, and to a long history of studying male bodies as a stand-in for all bodies.

ii. Contraception and Family Planning

> *'Parts of me are getting younger,*
> *scared of piss and tantrums and boys.'*
> *– 'A Speculative Script for Motherhood'*
> *by Emily Cotterill*

One area of healthcare which is central to twenty-first century Welsh women's lives is contraceptive and family planning services. Again, across the UK there seems to be a one-size fits all approach.

Oral contraceptives remain the most popular method of contraception in the UK. Given that the pill is simple, reliable and effective when used properly, it makes sense that it's also the first method GPs and sexual health clinics will suggest as a contraceptive. Synthetic hormones, however, are often a source of weight gain, depression, anxiety, loss of sex drive, acne and other symptoms in many women of reproductive age across the globe. In my own experience, and having spoken to numerous other women living in Wales, these potential side-effects aren't generally disclosed on consultation. At fourteen, I was handed the pill without so much as a conversation about the repercussions. At fifteen, I began taking antidepressants. I can't help but wonder if there is a correlation between pumping my body with artificial hormones, and a steep decline in mental health that continued for over a decade.

Research undertaken in Denmark found that women on hormonal contraceptives, including non-oral products such as a patch, vaginal ring or hormonal IUD, were fifty percent more likely to be diagnosed with depression six months later. Another study conducted by the same researchers found that women on hormonal contraceptives were twice as likely to attempt suicide, with a success rate three times higher than those not on hormonal contraceptives. The risk of depression and attempted suicide was particularly high in those age fifteen to nineteen – this age range may be more prone to the influence of hormonal signalling due to the still-developing nature of their brains.

At present, the only non-surgical contraceptive available to men is the condom, and, sixty years since the pill become available in the UK, despite successful clinical trials, we are still waiting for a male equivalent. Consequently, the burden of contraception inevitably falls to women all over the world. In search of a longer-term solution, many women turn to the coil.

Years ago, when I was living in Gloucestershire, I attempted to have an IUD fitted in a Sexual Health Clinic. Despite being considered routine, the procedure was a disaster – it was agonisingly painful and resulted in me losing consciousness. The pain was so intense, I remember crying out, my body drawing back sharply and involuntarily. Then I blacked out.

When I came to, unfamiliar faces swaying above me, the arrest bell ringing in my ears like an incessant gull, my dress was still hitched above my waist, my legs still spread open. As the blood returned to my brain, and my vision slowly came back into focus, I was shaken and sick.

Afterwards, friends poked fun at me and I wondered why I'd had such an awful experience compared to others. I've always been prone to fainting, and have a reputation for passing out cold during blood tests or at the mention of broken bones and other injuries. Add to that a slight tendency towards amateur dramatics, and it stands to reason it was all 'in my mind,' a problem with me and not the routine procedure, which the NHS website simply says 'can be uncomfortable.' Over the years, the event morphed in my mind – despite the very real distress I had experienced at the time, I assumed I must have a low pain threshold, or that I'd been at the hands of an inexperienced practitioner. The more women I spoke to who had nothing but positive remarks about the coil left me feeling like an anomaly, a drama queen, a wimp.

More recently, following the birth of my first son and having returned to Wales, I decided to try again. Sick to death of pumping my body with artificial hormones, I saw a copper IUD as my only option. This time, I spoke with a Health Visitor, who was honest about her own levels of discomfort during a coil fitting, but advocated for the device as a reliable and simple method of contraception. Although a little hesitant, I convinced myself that this time would be different – I had conquered a few phobias during pregnancy and childbirth, not even flinching at the routine blood tests or the IV drip I had in my hand during labour, and emerged feeling confident and empowered. I assumed the procedure would be less painful now that my cervix had been dilated naturally through childbirth, and assured myself that this time I'd have a more confident practitioner – it would be the 'slightly uncomfortable' five-minute procedure I'd read and heard about.

Unfortunately, it was not to be. Once again, the pain was unbearable. It was like an assault. Again, I cried out involuntarily, bucked, and passed out. Despite having given the doctor my permission to carry out the fitting,

I felt violated.[2] Later, the doctor explained that the process of stimulating the cervix stimulates the vagus nerve: vasovagal syncope, (fainting), occurs when the part of your nervous system that regulates heart rate and blood pressure malfunctions in response to a trigger, such as the sight of blood, but can also be triggered by stimulation of the nerve itself. She simply said, 'The coil is not for you.' I felt absolutely helpless and entirely out of options.

Again, some friends frustratingly suggested the issue was psychological, and I began to wonder why the experience was so much worse for me than for the majority of women. A little investigating and a sudden recent bout of media coverage on the issue has highlighted a few key things. In a study of nulliparous women, approximately seventeen percent reported severe pain associated with placement of a levonorgestrel-releasing intrauterine system.[1] In a study of mainly multiparous women, approximately eleven percent reported severe insertion-related pain. This is not an insignificant figure by any means, and yet the agonising pain that can occur during coil fittings is so rarely discussed as to be virtually unknown anecdotally – certainly I felt isolated following my experience, and was left struggling to impress upon others how truly painful I had found it, how traumatised I felt. On one

---

[2] Having read this essay, my husband, a medical practitioner himself, suggested 'assault' and 'violated' were over-dramatic terms, and that the use of these words would take away from the gravity of my experiences. I did not choose these descriptions lightly, and stand by them as my own truth of what I underwent during both procedures. Sadly, my husband's reaction has only served to solidify the medical bias I am examining in the context of this essay.

occasion, during a consultation regarding the morning-after pill, a well-meaning pharmacist even repeatedly suggested the coil as an alternative form of emergency contraception, despite me having explained the sheer impossibility of attempting the procedure for a third time.

Then something illuminating happened – in 2021, writer and broadcaster Caitlin Moran called for all women to be offered pain relief during coil fittings. She was shortly followed by BBC journalist Naga Munchetty, who spoke about her own 'coil fitting agony,' saying she felt 'violated, weak and angry.' For me, the article felt groundbreaking – the secrecy of the pain and shock associated with coil fittings for some women was finally shattered. I wasn't alone.

And so, I have come to realise I am not the only woman who has experienced this horrendous reaction, and yet there is very little being done in the way of improving the experience for women like me. At its core, this is an issue around how we consider and react to women's pain, particularly in healthcare settings. In fact, studies have shown that healthcare professionals' perception of patient pain during gynaecological procedures is not an accurate reflection of the patient's own pain experience. No wonder so many women feel dismissed when communicating their pain during IUD fittings.

iii. Maternity services

> *'I could have wished for a window*
> *a portal through muscle and blood, to watch*
> *you, acrobat, whispering to yourself*
> *I was scanning my whole body for newness.'*
> *– 'Window' by Rae Howells*

Failure to invest in mothers and caregivers is something that was highlighted to me during the Covid pandemic of 2020. That year, the Healthcare Inspectorate Wales published Phase 1 of its review of maternity services, in which sixteen and a half percent of women felt their wishes for birth were not listened to. Due to the Covid pandemic, Phase 2 was delayed, then scrapped altogether. Therein lies part of the problem. How can we hope for better when the research into what is working and what isn't is no longer being conducted?

Remember that first failed coil fitting? At the height of the crisis, I gave birth prematurely to my first son. I spent hours labouring alone before my husband was finally allowed to join me, and then spent a week on the postnatal ward while my tiny baby recovered in SCBU, with no visitors allowed. No family and no friends. No physical contact with anyone, apart from the coordinated illicit corridor visits with my husband, which took me right back to our school days, when we would covertly clasp hands in the hallways between classes. During this time, it became clear to me that within healthcare settings, women's needs were at the very bottom of the heap. Unfortunately this felt especially apparent in Wales (despite Bethan Sayed's attempts to raise awareness and campaign for change).

Throughout the pandemic, Wales had generally been confident in using its devolved powers to make and implement decisions ahead of Westminster, introducing border enforcement and national lockdowns separate to the rest of the UK, but new parents were massively overlooked amongst the creating and easing of Covid restrictions, particularly in healthcare settings. For women frantically searching an ultrasound for a heartbeat, pacing an antenatal ward alone, or sitting at their premature baby's incubator, there was no easing of restrictions, no compassion.

A friend of mine gave birth to her second child, her husband rushing into the room as the baby's head crowned, nearly missing the event entirely. A neighbour sat alone on a theatre bed, about to undergo an unplanned caesarean section. The midwife held her hand as she cried. In December 2020, I was thrilled to see that the NHS had finally changed its guidance to say women should be allowed to have a birthing partner there 'at all times' and not just for 'active labour' – a thrill that turned to disappointment when I saw that this applied only to birthing women in England. Despite campaigns and petitions, the issue fell on deaf ears in Wales, and at the time of writing this essay at the end of 2022, the presence of birthing partners and maternity visitors was still at the discretion of each health board in Wales, leaving the issue of crucial support during pregnancy, childbirth and afterwards down to a postcode lottery. Some women even felt pushed into electing for unnecessary caesarean sections in order to bypass the arbitrary 'active labour' rule and ensure they could have their partners present during the procedure, but even planned sections were left to the discretion of individual health boards and hospitals, meaning many women were alone until the point of the first incision.

Having spoken with others, I've been astounded by how much women are expected to endure under the medical sphere. This becomes especially apparent during pregnancy and birth, when so many women are rebranded as 'mum,' denied bodily autonomy and stripped of their choices. Part of the reason behind this may be that in healthcare settings, we instantly feel vulnerable. We don't realise that we have a choice, that we can question what practitioners are telling us, assess the benefits and risks and make our own decisions. We are often not even presented with the decisions. Not long ago, a friend described to me how a doctor and a midwife had stood beside her hospital bed discussing plans to begin an induction that she hadn't consented to (and ultimately didn't need). Countless women are pushed into unnecessary medical interventions, such as induction of labour and unplanned sections because of this, not realising that they can, in fact, say 'Thank you, but no thank you.'

Recently, a friend of mine was admitted to hospital with gallstones just three weeks after the birth of her little girl. She was kept as an inpatient for a week, during which time, because of ongoing Covid restrictions, she was not allowed to see her newborn baby. Unsupported by hospital staff, this meant she had to end her breastfeeding journey just three weeks in – far sooner than she had hoped. When the trauma, grief and heartache of this awful situation drove her to tears, a nurse accused her of 'being hormonal.'[3] Another friend who suffered a miscarriage at sixteen weeks, has been waiting on autopsy results for over two years – a wait which has had an effect on her ability to grieve, made all the more crucial as the results could have a bearing on subsequent pregnancies. She has been informed this delay is due to staffing issues, which can be partly attributed to both Brexit, and the endless cuts to our NHS instigated by Westminster. While healthcare in Wales is devolved, and funding is attributed at the discretion of the Welsh Government, we remain under the influence of the Barnett Formula, meaning that the amount of public expenditure allotted to the NHS in Wales is reflective of adjustments to public expenditure in England, despite the differing needs of both countries.

Depleting funding at the hands of Westminster has had a disproportionate effect on women's health and maternity care. Recent exposés have reported grim findings for trusts across England, with Shrewsbury and Telford, East Kent and Morecambe Bay all falling severely short of adequate care standards. Despite this, NHS England has dropped plans to improve the safety

---

[3] The anguish at being separated from her tiny baby aside, having given birth only three weeks previously, she was also absolutely entitled to be 'hormonal'.

of maternity care by ensuring women are seen by the same team of midwives throughout pregnancy, labour and postnatal care. Thankfully, I saw the same fantastic community midwife throughout both my pregnancies, but as with many policies in Wales, the allocation of midwife care varies by health board, something the Welsh Government has the power to alter if they choose to do so.

iv. Postnatal and lactation support

> *'We fail together, over and over,*
> *[...] until my nipples are wounds*
> *and you are drinking blood.'*
> *— 'On Understanding the Gods'*
> *by Joanna Ingham*

Beyond pregnancy and birth, we enter the realm of postnatal support. During the Covid pandemic, this was abysmal – in fact, my first born had no contact with health care professionals beyond his routine vaccine appointments. While my second baby has had more contact, things still haven't been great. For the first eleven weeks of his life, he fed constantly. Not in the typical, newborn, 'feeding a lot' way, but in a truly relentless, insatiable way that meant that at any given time he was either nursing or crying. Eleven weeks is a long time to have a baby fixed to your breast. Meeting his needs alongside my toddler's was exceptionally challenging. It transpired a posterior tongue-tie was preventing him from feeding effectively, leading to near-constant hunger, centile loss, and poor sleep. Despite speaking with a health visitor, a child health nurse, and a GP, this tongue-tie was only discovered when I consulted with a breastfeeding charity and spoke with a wonderful voluntary IBCLC[4] who recognised the signs and rushed the referral through. Before my own experience, tongue-tie was a condition I was unfamiliar with – I had no idea what to look out for; no idea that he was anything other than a very hungry and unsettled baby.

You'd be forgiven for thinking otherwise as they are the first point of contact for breastfeeding mothers, but Health Visitors and midwives only receive a minimal amount of training in breastfeeding and lactation; around eighteen hours in total. Breastfeeding knowledge and practical skills vary widely among healthcare professionals, with peer supporters, breastfeeding counsellors and IBCLCs often undertaking their own training and volunteering with charities to provide women with the support they so desperately need. There are only a handful of qualified IBCLCs in Wales. This isn't surprising – qualifying as an IBCLC involves five years of training, for which there is limited funding available. Naturally, this has pushed many Wales-based practitioners into the realms of private practice, which could prevent anyone without the finances from seeking support, resulting in mothers who are unable to feed, and ultimately grieving the premature end to their breastfeeding journey.

In the National Review of Maternity Services Survey, published in October 2020 by Wavehill, two thirds of

---

[4] IBCLC – International Board Certified Lactation Consultant.

those who responded to questions around breastfeeding support reported negative experiences, including poor-quality advice and the absence of support. This is absolutely an area which needs investment, for the sake of women's mental and emotional health, as well as for the physical wellbeing of new mothers and their babies. Interestingly, the Welsh Government introduced a Five Year Breastfeeding Plan in 2019, designed to improve understanding of, and support for, breastfeeding. Unfortunately, there doesn't seem to have been much quantifiable change as a result of this well-intentioned strategy. Perhaps redistribution of healthcare workers during the Covid pandemic played a part in waylaying these plans, but chronic staff shortage is also an issue.[5] A more serious concern is the misinformation still relayed by healthcare professionals – take, for example, a nurse who recently incorrectly advised a friend to begin formula feeding her baby, claiming that the antibiotics she was prescribed for mastitis were not safe for breastfeeding.

The consequence of this chronic lack of funding and interest is that the UK and Ireland regularly have the lowest breastfeeding rates in the entire world. Only 0.5% of babies in Wales and England are breastfed beyond the first year, compared with 23% in Germany, 27% in the USA and 56% in Brazil. Anecdotally, it seems that often the intention is there, but the support is severely lacking, with thousands of women having to stop before they feel ready, or turn to

---

[5] When my first born turned 15 months, despite having never received a routine health visitor appointment, we were simply sent a letter stating his 15-month check would not go ahead due to lack of available staff.

private practice for support. 'Lactation failure' is not a diagnosis we should accept – when billions are spent on erectile dysfunction, lactation issues should have the same focus, but we remain, as ever, at the mercy of policy makers who devalue this experience for mothers and babies.

v. Menopause

> *'The doctor says it's nothing serious, something*
> *she'll just have to live with, a malfunction*
> *[...] not uncommon in women*
> *of her age.'*
>
> > – *'Burning Mouth Syndrome'*
> > *by Victoria Gatehouse*

From around the age of forty-five, women may begin to experience symptoms of the menopause, typically associated with hot flashes, poor sleep, thinning hair, weight gain and mood changes, amongst other symptoms.

Discomfort can be managed through a combination of lifestyle changes and hormonal treatment, but before reduced symptoms can become a reality for women, we must ensure there is adequate awareness in the general population, as well as sufficient recognition and training in the medical field. While several workplaces run menopause cafes and support groups, these tend to be organised by the employees themselves, rather than spear headed by employers.

In 2021, Davina McCall made waves with her documentary 'Sex, Myths and the Menopause', resulting in a significant surge in demand for HRT. While Wales continues to use its devolved powers to offer free prescriptions to its inhabitants, including prescriptions for HRT, those living in England must still pay for their medication. A recent report by the All-Party Parliamentary Group on Menopause has recommended scrapping prescription charges for HRT in England, as is the case in all devolved nations. UK-wide recommendations from the APPG also included ensuring doctors are trained on menopause (scandalously, most aren't), and summoning all women over forty-five to the GP to discuss the menopause. I would suggest that these conversations need to happen sooner – there are women younger than forty-five who are impacted by experiences of menopause or peri menopause. In fact, if there were better awareness and more open discussion across all areas, perhaps the need for an individual GP consultation would be negated. This brings us back to the need for thorough, accurate sex education for both sexes and all genders, beginning in school.

While prescription rates doubled in the richest areas of the UK following the Channel 4 documentary, in the most deprived areas, only half as many women have received the treatment, demonstrating a massive discrepancy between affluent women and those living in more difficult financial circumstances. A recent Newson Health survey found that 23% of women who reported symptoms of menopause were prescribed antidepressants, rather than HRT, against NICE guidelines. This is yet another example of women being diagnosed with mental health issues when the problem is rooted in the physical.

Better education, understanding and support for menopausal women is not just something that would benefit half the population. Studies have shown that the long-term neglect of the menopause in our health sector is costing the UK economy £10bn, as women often leave their jobs during this challenging, yet unavoidable time in their lives. The direct effects on the NHS are also significant – around half the NHS workforce is aged forty-five or above, and 77% are female. According to Kate Muir, if one in ten menopausal women in the NHS leave their jobs, as is the case in the wider UK population, retaining those staff would save the health service around £700m. Despite the case for a total policy-reform regarding the menopause, recent proposals to change UK legislation to protect the rights of women experiencing menopause have been in part rejected by the government due to fears such a move would discriminate against men. The government also rejected calls for a large-scale pilot of 'menopause leave' in England. While case law in Wales dictates medical information must be taken into account, there is no specific legislation addressing the impact of the menopause in the workplace. Incidentally, Spain has very recently become the first European country to pass a paid 'menstrual leave' law. Perhaps other countries will follow suit and consider the impact of the menopause as well as menstruation.

Despite an increase in funding due to extra spending on the NHS in England, recent budget reports suggest the Welsh Government won't be apportioning all that extra amount to our already cash-strapped health services, choosing instead to invest elsewhere. Of course, our powers as a devolved nation only go so far – we are still at the mercy of the Barnett Formula; a construct that limits our abilities by allocating funding on the basis of decisions made on the political whim of a group who aren't close to the needs of those of us who make Wales our home. So what can we do?

What we need is truly inclusive conversations around women's biology, from the symptoms and effects of the menstrual cycle to the menopause. Timing is key here – this information needs to be embedded earlier, with education regarding what to expect needed for both sexes. The status quo regarding sex education has resulted in generations of people, including medical professionals, who do not understand their own bodies. I can't think of better proof that the medical industry is still rife with outdated and outrageous views about women's anatomy than this: it is 2023, and in medical schools, 'virgin speculum' is still the term used to refer to the extra small speculum used for smear tests. Fundamentally, virginity is a social construct with no biological reality, and yet myths about the hymen still abound, and in some cases women are being denied scans or probes in the interest of 'preserving' their virginity.

The devolution of education in Wales has given the Welsh government the power to introduce the aforementioned change to the curriculum around sexual education. We are educating the next generation – those who will be developing and implementing new legislation and framework in years to come, as well as those who

45

will be working in healthcare settings. While healthcare also remains devolved, given that women and their access to fair and equitable treatment are generally at the mercy of policy makers and their funding decisions, it's imperative that we teach our children that the male body is not the default or norm by which we should set our standards, but rather merely representative of *half* the population. That women's pain is valid and real; that what may be a perfectly acceptable experience for one woman may be horrific for another (see: the coil and smear tests); and that every female patient deserves the same consideration and compassion afforded to their male counterparts. Let's teach our children that the time for women to keep their words in is over. Let's make our voices heard, in Wales and beyond.

Bibliography

'Act Now To Tackle Unmet Need: Newson Health Responds To Menopause All-Party Parliamentary Group Report – Balance Menopause,' Balance Menopause. https://www.balance-menopause.com/news/act-now-to-tackle-unmet-need-newson-health-responds-to-menop ause-all-party-parliamentary-group-report/ [accessed 18 March 2023].

All Wales Breastfeeding Five Year Action Plan. 2019. https://www.gov.wales/sites/default/files/publications /2019-06/all-wales-breastfeeding-five-year-action-plan-july-2019_0.pdf [accessed 18 March 2023].

ALL WALES MENOPAUSE POLICY. 2019. (Public Health Wales) [accessed 18 March 2023].

Bahamondes, Luis, Diana Mansour, Christian Fiala, Andrew M Kaunitz, and Kristina Gemzell-Danielsson, 'Practical Advice for Avoidance of Pain Associated with Insertion of Intrauterine Contraceptives', *J Fam Plann Reprod Health Care, 40.1: 54–60*, 2024 https://doi.org/10.1136/jfprhc-2013-100636

'Coil Fitting Agony: "My Screams Were So Loud"', BBC News, 2021. https://www.bbc.co.uk/news/health-57551641 [accessed 18 March 2023].

Billock, Jennifer, 'Pain Bias: The Health Inequality Rarely Discussed', BBC Future, 2018. https://www.bbc.com/future/article/20180518-the-inequality-in-how-women-are-treated-for-pain [accessed 18 March 2023].

'Breastfeeding In The UK'. 2023. <https://anya.health/breastfeeding-uk/ [accessed 18 March 2023].

Burgess, Anna, Chloe Maughan, Mallika Kshatriya, Eddie Knight, and Llorenc O'Prey. Maternity Services Survey, October 2020 (Wavehill), 2023. https://www.hiw.org.uk/sites/default/files/2020-11/Wavehill MaternityServicesSurveyEN.pdf [accessed 18 March 2023].

Halpern Prince, Jenny, 'The "Virgin Speculum": Proof That Medicine Is Still Rife With Outrageous Myths About Women', the *Guardian*. https://www.theguardian.com/commentisfree/2023/jan/19/virgin-speculum-medicine-outrageous-myths-women-cervical-screenings-british [accessed 18 March 2023].

'Health,' European Institute For Gender Equality. https://eige.europa.eu/gender-mainstreaming/policy-areas/health [accessed 18 March 2023].

Heredia, Carmen, 'Large Danish Study Links Contraceptive Use To Risk Of Depression', *Kaiser Health News*, 2016. https://khn.org/news/large-danish-study-links-contraceptive-use-to-risk-of-depression/ [accessed 18 March 2023].

'It Takes An Average 7.5 Years To Get A Diagnosis Of Endometriosis – It Shouldn't', Endometriosis UK. [n.d.]. https://www.endometriosis-uk.org/it-takes-average-75-years-get-diagnosis-endometriosis-it-shouldnt [accessed 18 March 2023].

'The Ripples Of Trauma Caused By Severe Pain During IUD Procedures – , *The BMJ*, 2021. https://blogs.bmj.com/bmj/2021/07/20/the-ripples-of-trauma-caused-by-severe-pain-during-iud-procedures/ [accessed 18 March 2023].

'Minister Lee Waters Calls Female Opponent's Remarks Hysterical', BBC News, 2022. https://www.bbc.co.uk/news/uk-wales-politics-63731075 [accessed 18 March 2023].

Muir, Kate. 2022. 'It's The Menopause, Stupid – Why Britain Can't Afford To Ignore Women's Health', the *Guardian*, 2022. https://www.theguardian.com/ commentisfree/2022/oct/17/menopause-britain-women-health-economy [accessed 18 March 2023].

'Welcome to 28ish Days Later', BBC Radio 4. 2022. https://itunes.apple.com/podcast/id1614435903 [accessed 18 March 2023].

'Who's Who In Breastfeeding Support And Lactation In The UK,' LCGB. https://lcgb.org/why-ibclc/whos-who-in-breastfeeding-support-and-lactation-in-the-uk/?fbclid =IwAR2Qi-0rXlxOE46UQbt4tHOZF58eASh 3pv18ni4KfL6uXuMgGeXSKBDtHCU [accessed 18 March 2023].

OCCUPIED SPACES: PUBLIC LIFE AND MARGINALISED BODIES IN WALES

By Grace Quantock

I know I'm the first, because they tell me so.

'You're the first one we've had,' is a pervasive refrain whenever I enter professional spaces. But everyone's excited for me to be a guinea pig so they can find out if their wheelchair ramps, you know – actually work.

This is how it used to go, all too often: I was in a board room; ferociously clean, lots of glass, top floor, lifts keyed to stop only at the level your passkey grants access to and such intense security I'd got trapped in the lobby after going to the loo. From the floor-to-ceiling windows I could see a skyline cluttered with steel and wealth all around. The vertiginous view was disconcerting. I was wearing a navy French Connection dress that cut sharply across my collar bones. I bought it at a charity shop, in hope of work that would require such a dress.

An upper-class White man was telling me how diverse and inclusive the work under discussion was. Apparently, he was 'diverse' – it's diversity of thought that counts, I was told.

'Oh yes, I'm all for diversity,' he assured us. 'There's a woman on one of my boards, a Black woman. She's a full board member you know.' The tone of surprise. I blinked, trying to comprehend the skewed logic of his

51

statement. The other older White men around the table nodded, as though this was a reasonable comment. I started to speak but he rolled on, 'Oh yes, well, her father was very important in the industry, you know. So she has a lot to contribute.'

'Why would you need to point out a Black woman is a full board member? Why would you need to tell us what her father does?' I asked.

'Perhaps it's relevant, we don't know,' a man to my left admonished me.

I was the only woman, the only disabled person, the only working-class person in the room. Perhaps the only one that had ever been in the room – it certainly felt like it in that moment.

I wondered what their fathers did. I don't think my father needs to earn me a place around the board table. But how are those places earned and who gets to speak and to listen when it comes to our country's healthcare, social care, arts, digital infrastructure and human rights? Public appointments oversee vast swathes of public life – public bodies spend over £200 billion a year of taxpayer's money. Ranging from NHS boards, to Arts Council, Chair of the BBC, to prison monitoring boards. These public appointees' work shapes all our lives. I didn't grow up knowing this, while I learned (a bit) about governments in school. I'd never realised public bodies functioned in so much of our daily lives.

I was in my mid-twenties when I saw an advert asking for new board members that asked 'Are you under 30, a woman, LGBT, BAME? We need you!'. I was working as a ghost writer and copy writer, and helping a local public health organisation by ghosting their internal newsletter. But when I saw the advert, I realised I fit most of those criteria, so I applied for my first public body role. I didn't get a job on the board, but now that I'd discovered organisations like this existed and meetings were open to the public, I kept attending. I sat in the public gallery with the journalists, who filled me in on who was who and caught me up on all the controversies. I learned how to ask questions that held people accountable and how to phrase my point in a way that elicited an answer.

I really began working for public bodies because I was told I couldn't. The leader of the body I first applied to told me someone like me would never get chosen to join a board. Exactly what 'like you' meant wasn't made clear. I asked, of course. I wondered if they were objecting to me being a woman, under thirty, working class, disabled, neurodivergent or any of the other intersections of identities I sit within. He asked if I could see myself being appointed to the board of British Airways. This was offered as a ridiculous suggestion. But I think BA could benefit from my insight – it might help them break fewer wheelchairs, at least. We might tackle some of their other pervasive problems too, like their carbon emissions. But in that room, it was just me, the head of the public body and his second-in-command.

'Welsh government always tell us they want people like this,' he continued. 'People with... protected... racial characteristics.' He stumbled over unfamiliar phrasing.

'Protected racial characteristics? Do you actually know

any people of colour?' I asked. 'I don't mean, do they serve you coffee, but do you actually work with anyone who isn't just like you?'

He ignored me and continued speaking. 'Yes, the government always ask for them, but in reality, they never get to interview.'

I wondered why he was being so frank with me. I don't know if this man thought himself untouchable or if he just thought I didn't know any journalists. It's okay though, I sold the story to the *Guardian* soon after (then I was appointed to a national board which I was told had the highest number of applicants for a public body role in Welsh Government history). I've been told since that the man now tells people I'm his protege. I'm not sure he knows me well enough to realise how much he's risking his conservative reputation by claiming that, but maybe he doesn't read the *Guardian*, so perhaps he won't be unduly disturbed by what I do. The comfort of people who despise me isn't my concern. Instead, I'm working to shift the landscapes of public life enough to be representative of the people we are here to serve. I'm not a career board member; I'm a therapist, writer and researcher who sits on boards across health and social care. This means that I'm at board one day, trying to influence national decisions and policy, and the next day I'm sitting with people at the tough end of the decisions made at a national level.

In the current board landscape, I'm often the first disabled person older colleagues may have met in a professional contact. I shouldn't be, but this is institutionalisation's legacy – how uncomfortable many non-disabled adults are with disabled people, because when they grew up we weren't visible, because we weren't free. Asylums and group homes are not really so long ago. It's not only in the trauma inflicted in the homes, but the contributions of disabled people that were missed, the older people now learning to live on the outside. The shadow of institutionalisation impacts everyone. If they've never really spoken to a disabled person before, or realise there's nobody disabled living in their street, then that's an impact. Institutionalisation's shadow impacts my body in the majority of spaces today.

Perhaps many people don't see themselves as pitying me. The charity model of disability sees disabled people as poor victims of circumstance in need of help and sympathy, as opposed to humans with rights and access needs. This resistance to access extends beyond disability; a person with a baby needing space for a buggy, childcare leave and a creche is often framed as an inconvenience – we don't give them the access they deserve either. I speak in board rooms, on train platforms, on stages; bracing myself for cloying sympathy, the chloroform of pity, knowing I am being harmed in sharing, but speaking out because I hope to stop harm to those coming up behind me.

Let's take an example: I needed to get the train to a board meeting, a forty-five-minute journey. The line was being repaired and the rail replacement coaches were not wheelchair accessible. I asked for an accessible bus or taxi, which was not well received. When I shared the experience online, I was tone-policed, instructed to: 'Always remember to thank staff that go above and beyond to help.' Here's the thing: I don't want me getting to work on time to be something that necessitates underpaid staff having to 'go above and beyond'. I don't want help, but access.

If staff take time to help me – because the system isn't designed for disabled passengers, so they are working around it – then that time has to come from somewhere. I'm not comfortable with staff cutting their break time to get me to my destination.

It also means I can't just be another passenger, I have to be 'grateful' for help. Do you know how tiring it is to always be in another's debt, always demonstrating appropriate thankfulness? It's so expected of disabled people, of immigrants, of any marginalised person in a space we've historically been excluded from. The spaces aren't really built for us yet because in real terms, we haven't been allowed access to such public and professional spaces for very long.

I don't even have to say anything, I just have to turn up and need to use the loo.

'It's totally accessible, there's just a small step. Derek here will carry you over it.'

'Uh, no, I'm not going into a bathroom with Derek, sorry.'

'Oh, and the lightbulb is out, no one here uses it, you see. But you can wee in the dark, right?'

'No, my aim isn't that good.'

'Look, can you move around the boxes in here? We use

it as storage as we don't have anyone like you here. If you'd rung and warned us, we would have turned on the stairlift, wouldn't we?'

The role of public bodies has shifted and renewed throughout devolution in Wales. After devolution, there was a focus on Welsh Government reclaiming power, a move towards transparency and a push for inclusion for arms-length bodies. In 2004 Rhodri Morgan, First Minister, announced that the Welsh Development Agency, Wales Tourist Board, and education quango Elwa, would become part of his government by 2006. 'Today marks the end of the quango state as we have known it,' he told the assembly. It was his 'bonfire of quangos.' But the functions of public bodies still exist, often under different names, or in different places. In researching the history of devolution and public bodies, I found many instances of governments – particularly new governments – announcing overhauls or bonfires of public bodies. It's a well-loved image; the cutting through red tape, the bonfire of waste and the reclamation of control by a central government. In April 2022, Jacob Rees-Mogg announced an overhaul of 'increasing' numbers of quangos, with plans to shut or merge many, following similar comments made by Blair, Brown and Truss.

I believe good governance is essential and transparency is necessary for a functioning democracy. But the announcements which only occasionally translate into action beyond the headlines feel a little to me like the government promises that we can see our GPs within two weeks. Perhaps necessary, but much more complex to deliver than to promise. The issue of long GP waiting times isn't an issue of inefficiency or lack of motivation but a complex web of issues around recruitment, retainment of medics, retirement age of the current cohort, the increasing complexity of needs for the average GP appointment and environmental factors meaning people are needing more help and have less resources.

This was a question I raised at a public board meeting recently when the UK government announced plans to publish league table style reports of GP waiting times. It was said to be informing patients by publishing data on how many appointments each GP practice delivers and that the length of waits for appointments would enable patient choice. I asked how will that enable patient choice? If my GP has long waiting times, will this data be part of a policy allowing me to easily choose a different GP? Will it take into account complexity of appointment times and take-up in socio-economically disadvantaged areas? The answer was to allow patients to have data and to ask their GP practice why they are not doing better.

The concept of increasing data transparency and access is great. The reality of whether this will get people seen sooner is questionable. If I was trying to get people into a GP appointment quickly, I'm not sure increased data is the most direct route. While this occupied headline space, it didn't lead to action or reduced waiting times. Such energy and attention could have been spent on a policy that listened to what patients needed and co-created a solution with their doctors.

Devolution has impacted health decisions in Wales in

many ways, from free prescriptions, free senior and disabled public transport, to organ donation. But more diverse voices are necessary for Wales's future. I sit on the boards of Social Care Wales, where I chair Regulation and Standards, I'm Vice-Chair of Citizen's Voice Body and I've sat on the boards of Digital Health and Care Wales and the Equality and Human Rights Commission. As a graduate of the pilot Equal Power Equal Voice programme, a cross-equalities public life mentoring scheme for marginalised people, I see the talent that can contribute to public life in Wales.

When I first discovered boards existed, I knew I wanted to contribute to the conversation, but I didn't know how. My first interview for a health board had over 250 applicants and people flew in to interview. I was the only person in the room who wasn't a mayor, a former head of social services or a retired 'captain' of industry. Or at least, that's what it felt like then. I was also the only visibly disabled person in the room, the only one under thirty and one of a handful of women. I didn't get that role and I knew I needed support to understand the complex landscape and to navigate it as a woman with multiple marginalised identities.

Many public bodies seek corporate, financial sector or senior executive backgrounds in board recruitment. Beginning in public office, I felt very aware of not having such a background. Structural and psycho-emotional disablism can create fragmented CVs and curtail career building. Due to the impact of disability, my CV is non-traditional – often not what public bodies are looking for.

In my board work, I find seeing the concepts come into action most rewarding. It's the moment where policy meets people. My work has always been about people; their narratives, needs, restoration, resources and potential for change. That's work I am continuing at board level: I hope to contribute my unique lived, governance and professional experience.

The number of disabled people in public roles may be going down, but the data for disability is complicated. We know in 2020, just 5.8% of new appointments were made to disabled people, down from 6% in 2019. In most recent data, just 5.0% of new public appointees report a disability, through the new question asked by The Office for Commissioner of Public Appointments, which has changed the way it gathers information about disability. There have also been big setbacks in representation of women, returning to the level of eight years ago. People from ethnic minority backgrounds have also got fewer appointments, with only 9.6% appointed in 2021. This means our lives are being impacted by people who don't represent us, those they are there to serve. But one in five people in the UK consider themselves disabled, including mental health issues, long-term health conditions and people with learning disabilities, according to the One in Five campaign who are calling for more disabled politicians. Which means we would need sixty-five disabled MPs to be representative of the number of disabled people living in the UK.

'Ultimately, this is only a question of talent,' explained Lord Holmes of Richmond, a disabled peer, who led a Parliamentary Review into opening up public appointments to disabled people in 2018. 'All of that bright, brilliant talent, resting within disabled people up and down the country. If you have the leadership, the culture and the unstinting commitment to go and seek out and connect with all of that talent, you will get to a far better place, and a far better result.'

I contributed to the Lord Holmes Review. It found only 180 disabled people in public office out of around 6,000 public appointments. Public appointments are significant positions that have an impact on all our lives but are not often visible. Collectively public appointees are responsible for impact across healthcare, education, sport and the arts, energy, security and defence. But the proposals of the review have not been carried out. The number of disabled people in public roles has declined, with only forty-three appointed in 2019/2020. The Holmes review set a target of 11.3% disabled public appointees by 2022. It has not been reached.

Many disabled people are not in public life, or in public at all. Disability hate crime is increasing and making communities less and less safe. Over 9,250 disability hate crimes were reported to police across England and Wales last year, with around half classed as violent – involving assault or possession of weapons. This is up 4.4% from the previous twelve months, according to data from Freedom of Information Requests from the thirty-nine police forces across England and Wales. Violence against disabled women specifically has increased by a third since 2014.

Disabled women are almost twice as likely to be sexually assaulted than non-disabled women. Disabled women are also twice as likely to experience domestic abuse. I'm at risk from the same kinds of violence non-disabled women face, but I'm also at risk of abuse specific to disabled women, which can happen in 'a wider range of places and is enacted by more kinds of perpetrators' according to the Centre for Disability Studies, University of Leeds. This violence can include hate crimes, attacks on disabled women when they are most vulnerable such as during pregnancy or after a new diagnosis, and institutional violence from carers or from assistants required for help and support at home.

The advocacy group, Stop Hate UK, report that over 9,208 disability hate crimes were reported to the police across England and Wales in 2020/2021. They point out that disabled people face exacerbated difficulties in an already inaccessible world. Inaccessibility in housing, transport, infrastructure and information impacts social protection and puts disabled women at further risk. Violence against disabled women has increased by a third since 2014. Yet Disabled Survivors Unite, a UK support and advocacy group, point out there has been a drop in rape prosecutions and call for changes in the treatment of disabled survivors who report sexual violence to police. Many disabled women have spoken of the traumatising experience of being harmed by ableism, interrogation and dismissal by police, during their complaint process.

This all comes as cost of living soars, more people fall into fuel poverty and the disability pay gap stands at 13%. This means a disabled person earns 13% less than a non-disabled person in the same job, with equal qualifications and experience. This number rises to over 33% for autistic people. But life costs you £583 more on average a month if you're disabled, according to research by the disability charity Scope. The crisis in social care and mounting NHS waiting lists means that many people are struggling with increased pain and difficulty while waiting for treatment delayed by the pandemic.

To the best of my knowledge, in some of my roles I'm the youngest person holding that role in the UK, often the first disabled person. I want it to be that this isn't special or notable, but the baseline. I am lucky enough to be a part of supporting equitable, accessible life in Wales with transparency and engagement. Times are tough, we have so many urgent issues to attend to, from violence against women and girls to climate emergency and many more. But I know, to tackle these, it will take all of us. I'm so proud to be working to make sure our voices can be heard, and we are at the table when our futures are being decided. It's urgent. We have too little time, and there is too much talent to waste.

'WE'RE BUILDING SOMETHING'

By Krystal S. Lowe

I'm sitting here, at 23:07, next to a snoring five-year-old and beneath a dim lamp wondering how I got here. Which path, which choices, led me here? Looking back is always interesting, however, as I sit, with Young Lowe at my side. I feel an unshakable pull to look forward instead; to the purpose of all I'm working towards; all I'm building. I always say to Young Lowe, 'we're building something'. This is what allows me to continue when things are difficult, it's what allows me to make sacrifices, it's what drives me. This thing we're building, because Young Lowe is a part of this too, is our purpose in all we do.

I didn't always live here, a fact I proudly display. I grew up on a 21-square-mile fish hook in the middle of the Atlantic ocean. An island, well, an archipelago. Only 65,000 people live on over one hundred teeny, tiny islands sewn together by bridges and causeways.

In January 1990 I was born. The third daughter to a man who fought fires and a young woman who wrote stories. Canary was what he called me – because my yellow skin was a reminder of the canary bird. Although, unlike that beautiful yellow bird, bushy eyebrows framed my thin face where large ears stuck out from. I had thick dark brown curls, skinny legs and too long arms. All of which is still true – except for the legs which now more resemble a runner's than the ballet dancer I have become. When I was seven years old, I attended my first ballet/tap class in a small studio down the steps of Chancery Lane. And from that day on, I never stopped dancing. I assume as they lower my coffin into the earth, it will be rocking side to side from the motion radiating from my very bones.

So, I bet you want to know how I came here? To the sea of lush greenery that is Wales. Well, I made a choice. I chose to be a ballet dancer; instead of all the other things there are in this world to become. Being that I have dual citizenship, in a small bedroom in a bright green bungalow in the centre of that fish hook I Googled, 'Ballet companies in the UK.' I found many, of course, but it was Ballet Cymru that stood out to me the most. So, I joined. Kidding; it wasn't that easy. However, after two years and many tears, I joined Ballet Cymru as a company dancer and remained with them for eight years.

Choice. It's an odd thing. It's easy to feel we have no choice. But we do, and even the very tiniest choices lead to big change. Now, ten years into my career in dance, I choose to title myself: dancer, choreographer, writer, and director. They are many things, in one. I create dance theatre works for stage, public space, and film.

When I first started my career, I was a ballet dancer, and over the years, I have tagged on label after label. I refuse to refer to myself as 'multidisciplinary'. I find it ambiguous. And there is nothing I dislike more than ambiguity.

Over the years, I realised there was a theme to my work: values. Over the years, I realised that the choices I made in my work were the same choices I made in my life because their fuel was the same. My work explores themes of intersectional identity, mental health and wellbeing and empowerment, because my values centre authenticity, equity, innovation, and empowerment. My entire vision for my work and for this world are one and the same: 'equitable arts experiences that represent us all'. This is what I'm building. I build by collaborating with a wide diversity of communities, creatives and organisations who align with those values, with that vision, and who are keen to come along with me on this mission.

What's Most Important?

What is MOST important to you? Did you think I was talking to you? No, that is constantly my question for myself. 'Krystal, what is MOST important to you?' This is an essential question for yourself; not once, but regularly.

In Wales, in 2024, there are far more opportunities as a dance practitioner than as a dance performer and choreographer. I love being a dance practitioner; I chose Ballet Cymru for the vast amount of work they do facilitating workshops with people all over the UK. Through my work with Ballet Cymru I have met thousands of incredible people – all excited about dancing at the start or by the end of the session. However, what is most important to me is performance. There was a point in my career that I realised I was doing way more teaching, producing, facilitating, and speaking than dancing and I had to shout this question at myself: 'Krystal, what is MOST important to you?'. It's easy to be more focused on what will make the most money over what is most important – especially as a single mother. Above all that matters to me in my work, is Young Lowe. However, I must remain true to the woman, the artist that I am as well, and I fervently believe that this is possible. To be both a committed, responsible, and loving parent *and* a champion to your purpose as an artist.

So, at the end of 2021, I sat down next to my laptop and I made a calendar for that entire year – and I colour-coded it. Yes, I am that woman. I colour-code, I plan, I budget. Everything that involved me performing or dancing I coloured green (that's my favourite colour), everything that was me creating work through writing or choreographing was coloured a vibrant orange (I love vibrancy), producing was pale blue and on and on. Because after I made the choice of what was most important to me, I needed to back myself up with a simple and quick way of ensuring I stuck with it. Now, whenever I look at that calendar and there's not much green or orange, I stop taking on anything but dancing and making opportunities. And you know, an odd thing happens when you focus on what you want: you begin to see more of it. Wait, no. Not want. It's passion. While want matters, it doesn't matter most to me. If I only did what I wanted I'd probably sit in bed all day watching movies with buttered popcorn. Want is fragile. I do not make choices based on what I want to do, I make them based on what I am passionate about. To build upon want will only leave your foundation to crumble when the load gets too heavy. What I build on is passion – and I am very passionate.

In focusing myself on building from passion, and working well when I received opportunities, and being extremely strategic in my planning and promoting, I received what I am passionate about. I also realised I had to focus on what I feel I need to say as an artist, what I wanted to share with the world, and what I wanted to change in the world.

I started with me.

I am a Black, neurodivergent woman. I am many things in one. I started with my own identity. I wanted to share myself with the world as a means of connecting with it. As a means of allowing others who share my same characteristics to feel seen in the world. I started with my intersectional identity and made the choice to share it, authentically, with others and to acknowledge their intersectionality in my work as well. I aim to consider intersectional diversity in all I do, because none of us are just one thing.

As I create work more and more, I'm beginning to explore how I present myself on stage and in writing. And I'm beginning to question, 'Am I able to separate myself from my neurology?' and, 'Should I separate myself from my neurology'. If I'm performing, and I'm required to make a lot of eye contact, how do I approach this? When I write characters for myself, am I writing them as neurodivergent or neurotypical? Can I write a neurotypical character? Can I play a neurotypical character? And above all of this is the overarching question: should I? Should I erase a fundamental aspect of my identity? The obvious answer is, no, of course not. I should be all of me, in my fullness. However, the presentation of that obvious answer isn't nearly as straightforward. In a world where unmasking neurodivergent traits can be dangerous, many people, divergent and typical alike, haven't seen a fully free neurodivergent person. So what happens then, when they see them on stage? When they work with them in the studio space and hear, 'No, I can't look into their eyes without anxiety, so I won't.' They resist. That's what happens. And as a result, I resist displaying myself as a fully free neurodivergent woman.

In this sector, where we speak widely about striving for equity, diversity, and inclusion, what does accountability look like? Who are we accountable to, and who holds us accountable? I could spend my entire career seeking accountability and safe spaces and freedom to present as I am and never see the sector transform as fully as it should. But, I hold the power to do these things for myself and others. And when I ask myself who I am accountable to, my answer is those values that I've carefully developed to underpin all I do. I am accountable to myself. And so, in the investigation of whether or not to suppress my neuro-type, I've concluded, I don't. I show myself in the fullness of me and allow all audiences the incredible experience of a fully free neurodivergent person.

Who I Really Am

And every day I paint,
Diligently, carefully, I paint myself new.
And what is seen by others is this mess of colour,
And uneven lines.
But what I am becoming through the confusion,
And mess,
Is me.

And every day I paint,
Diligently,
Carefully,
I paint myself new.
I paint myself free.
Not hiding,
But revealing who I really am.
How?
With my fingertips I take off all that's same,
And reveal all that's rare.
I reveal who I really Am.
Because as the
'Master of my fate',
I get to choose which colours I paint with,
I get to choose who I really am,
I get to choose the person I become,
Because I am the artist who paints myself,
I am the maker of my own self.

And every day I paint,
Diligently,
Carefully,
I reveal for all to see
Who I really Am,
This is me.
And as I paint, I am freed.

I paint with my fingertips and I paint with my voice,
    and I paint with my movement.
Because through this art, I am me.

As I paint, I grow more vulnerable – more brave.
I paint, for me.

And every day I paint
because there is a part of me that so desperately seeks
    this sameness with those
around.
There is safety in the sameness.
There is.
Yet, I paint.
I paint to reveal who I really am, and I wear this paint
    to revolt against the sameness
that suffocates so sneakily.

Every day I paint,
Diligently, carefully –
I paint myself new.

Healthy Artist

My definition of a healthy artist is an artist who works in ways that are best for their mental health and wellbeing.

A healthy artist. Seems like an oxymoron. Is that possible – with all of the long hours, working weekends, self-doubt, and poor pay?

One of the most beautiful things about the arts is their potential to aid in the mental health and wellbeing of those who engage with it. Another artist once told me, 'The purpose of art is to entertain.' I completely disagree. I believe the purpose of art is to connect people – to themselves and each other. It is through this connection that we maintain mental health and wellbeing. It's for this reason that my work explores these themes.

Seven: The Elusive Experience of Being Whole

The clouds were pale grey – whipped by an anxious hand,
The wind blew silent and cold,
And the trees wobbled as drops of rain fell from their leafless branches.
The room – stood still –
Except for the subtle rise and fall of the lifeless mass,
Trying not to be noticed by the walls.
Faded blue fabric fell lazy over her devastated body.
Each inhale – a futile attempt at survival.

Suddenly, out of the silence,
The phone rings.

Limp faded fabric releases a pale, weak hand;
A hoarse voice speaks, 'Hello?'
And then nothing. More nothing.
Except the near-silent scratching of brittle bright red
nails
And then a tear-soaked throat
'Okay'.

There's the dizzy shuffling of piles of unclean clothes.
There's the curious sniffing of tops and socks.
There's the stumbling woman half-heartedly dressing.
There's the stifling of sobs while the wind thrashes
against the window.
Honey-brown eyes water her puffed cheeks;
As if those cheeks were barren soil eager to bear fruit.
And a devastated chest beats against a curtain of ebony
skin
Until the wearer of this curtain holds it tightly in.

A dark green Sedan opens its passenger door
And as the door opens her clenched fist pulls tighter
still.
Two women sit – silent and apart until one woman
reaches to the other.
The honey-eyed woman takes the bag and pulls out the
food.
A tortilla wrap filled with sausage, egg, potato, and red
sauce.
I have never seen a more disgusting combination.
The Sedan driver looks at me and begins to drive.

And as I eat that wrap, the parts of me that were
hollow – slowly warm.
The Sedan driver looks at me and I begin to cry.
Not because of the disgusting combination – but
because of the presence of the Sedan driver –
And I cover my tears with the usual, 'How are you?'
And the Sedan driver simply states, 'You don't have to
do that.'

'Seven' was created first as an autobiographical poem,
then a work-in-progress dance theatre piece before finally
being transformed into a short film script. That's what I
do, I take one idea and then I pull and pull on it until I
feel I've explored it in every context I can. In every
context I need, in order to find artistic release.

Whimsy, my dance theatre work for family audiences,
was first developed in 2014 as a children's story for me
to enjoy myself. Then, in 2019, in collaboration with
Jubilee Park Primary School year 6 pupils, funded by Arts
Council Wales, it was developed into a 25-minute piece
where the learners danced, acted, made costumes, and
played music. In the summer of 2019 Articulture Wales,
Arts Council Wales, and The Riverfront Theatre helped
Whimsy become a 15-minute English-language dance
theatre work for two performers. In 2020 I explored the
greater accessibility of Whimsy; in 2021 I researched and
developed a multilingual version of the work – performed
in British Sign Language, English, and Welsh; and finally,
in 2022 I self-published the work into a children's book,
illustrated by Cardiff-based artist Jessie Begum and

translated by Wales-based musician Kizzy Crawford; and performed the multilingual version of this dance theatre work at venues and festivals throughout Wales. You may be thinking, 'You must be finished now!', but no, I am not. Now, I am creating a next step in the series of 'Whimsy' with Theatr Genedlaethol Cymru, to be performed in Welsh and British Sign Language at venues all throughout Wales. And in the future, I'd love to develop *Whimsy* into a three-part animated mini-series.

So, why am I so dedicated and connected to *Whimsy*? She's me. She's a little girl who loves nature and easily sees the beauty in everything around her but struggles to see the beauty in herself. Through an adventure, she is able to see what's beautiful about her. And I wrote this story in order to support my mental health and wellbeing. And in sharing it, I'm able to support others to do the same.

Mental health and wellbeing aren't only themes with which I create my work but the process in which that work is created. This means flexible working hours and five-day work weeks; focusing on how things feel and what they mean to us instead of how things look; and paying people amounts that respect their time, energy, and experience.

Power

Power.
Power to stand.
Power to speak.
Power to protect.
Power to make change.

Power to change.
Power to support others.
Power to support ourselves.
Power in connection.
Power in us all.

I used to think power was an object
Held and pushed toward weak ones.
To ensure they felt it and saw it fully.
Then, and only then, would power be in full effect.
The object could be passed on,
One to another,
but never held by more than one person in any one space.

I used to think power was a weapon
That could be wielded at the bearer's hand
Only to demolish everything in its path, with a single
    command,
Leaving dust so small that no one would come against
    them again.

I used to think power was a place
That could be built up and tower over anyone in its
    shadow.
And when they tried to escape the darkness,
Power would build higher – Nothing to fear.

I once met a white woman who would clothe herself in
    black
In order to feel powerful in high places.

For this woman, black meant power –
But only when put on.
I wonder if she also found that ironic –
As she stared at me.
Black, stretching tightly over my body.
Black filling every crease and crevice of my limbs.
The irony isn't in the absence of power when clothed in
    black,
The irony is in the assumed power in the skin she was
    already in.

I once watched a woman, who sat in the middle of a
    bay –
When it was winter.
She held a giant milkshake in between her hands,
And she shivered.
She said it made her feel powerful to choose to be cold.
Sometimes power gets confused with control.

And now, what do you think?

I think power isn't an object, to be held, and given –
    passed.
I think power isn't a weapon –
Power doesn't control,
Power incites respect,
Not fear.
Accountability, justice –
Never revenge.
Power is a substance – an energy,

Embodied.
Power is mine.
I think power is mine too.
I think power is refined in the quiet, unending, nights
    filled with questions and hope
for a new day.
I think power is designed for only those with the most
    gracious minds.

I think power is yours.
I think power is yours too.
Because power isn't a colour.
No, power isn't a colour, it's a substance, an energy.
We won't run out of it – it's never lost.
True power is never lost.

Empowerment

Empowerment. That's the final theme I explore with my work, because in a world as broken as ours, people need to be empowered. I do this in a range of ways: integrating access, offering new people opportunities, facilitating dance and writing workshops, and through Our Voice Network | Rhywdwaith Ein Llais.

Integrated Access:

In all of my work, I seek to ensure accessibility for d/Deaf and/or disabled audiences is seamlessly and creatively integrated. This is not only an exciting challenge to constantly conquer, but it means that these audiences see that their access is integral to the art and the artist.

And thus, they are integral to the arts and artists.

Remarkable Rhythm is a dance theatre work exploring communication and connection; it explores how we connect with those most unlike ourselves. This work is a piece of visual storytelling with dance as the medium; and the audio description is integrated as text spoken by the performers while they dance. In this way, *Remarkable Rhythm* seamlessly and creatively integrates access for d/Deaf and blind audiences.

Offering Opportunities:

As a freelance artist, I'm able to take risks on new people during projects. 'New' meaning new to me and/or the arts sector, so I have no reference for how they will work. When I pull together the creative team for a project, I make sure to give opportunities to as many new people as possible. Giving roles and tasks they've never had before. It's fair to say that this isn't always easy; it comes with many bumps, and yet, I stand by this choice. Because without these same opportunities, I wouldn't have this career that I love so much.

Arts Practitioner:

I always ensure that I make time for my work as an arts practitioner. Through dance and creative writing, I facilitate workshops in schools, communities, and venues, to empower people of all ages, disabled and non-disabled to see the full potential they have as artists (professional and amateur) and to experience the mental health and wellbeing benefits of engaging in the arts.

Our Voice Network | Rhwydwaith Ein Llais

I founded Our Voice Network in 2020 to empower, develop, and platform artists of the Global Majority through professional development opportunities, showcasing events, and bursaries. Through this network, I mentor and support the development of artists year-round through Our Voice Bursary as well as those who have not been awarded bursaries. Our Voice is an annual informal gathering for sharing art practices and processes and connecting with other artists and communities. This work is voluntary and sometimes tedious, but I love every second of it because I have been inexplicably impacted by the support of other artists throughout my career.

These are my themes: intersectional identity, mental health and wellbeing, and empowerment. Each theme is connected, not separate. Each theme weaves together into a three-cord thread that strengthens the other while ensuring the whole person is supported and not simply aspects of the individual.

There's Room for Me Too

To The Sector I love,
there's room for me too.
My intellect, my experiences, my thighs and my dark
　　skin –
I'm not a threat to you.
My place is in every space where art is made and
　　performed.
My creativity and my work will only improve the world.
There's room for me too.

So don't offer the lowest wage but showcase me on
    every poster
while simultaneously hiding me at the back of every stage.
At every age I have something to offer, something to give.
I shouldn't have to prove that my work is of worth
simply because of differences you can't seem to see past.
There's room for me too.

You hide behind words like 'classical' as an excuse
to continue racism, ableism, sexism, and exclusion.
You say there's no room in the writing for someone who
    looks like me,
as if excluding difference isn't centuries' old;
an injustice created by the insecure
that for some strange reason we refuse to truly end.
Why have we allowed this system to continue to stand?
Tell the truth.
You prefer racism instead of change – don't you?

Hear me.
If your shows cannot showcase me – Write. New. Shows.

Don't call me lucky when I've earned all I have.
Don't tell me that my skin isn't an issue but the shape
    of my Black body is –
Black isn't just a colour, it's culture and frame,
and so much more even I'm still seeking to discover.
If you struggle to pronounce my name –
practise.
Don't require

me to change it – once again –
to fit the aesthetic you claim.

There's room for my identity too.

My identity isn't a trophy for you to hold above your
    head
so you can feel some sort of triumph
while I'm reduced to simply skin.
Simply skin.
There is more to me than simply skin.
Where do I begin?
I'm my mother's brown eyes,
And my father's high chin.
I'm the places I've been.
I'm the friends I've kept.
I'm the language I speak because it doesn't only belong
    to you.
Am nad ydyw'n perthyn i chi'n unig.
Mae lle i mi hefyd.

There's room for me.
Not 'women like me' –
part of a community or group as if I have no individual
    identity.
Look at me
and see
the fullness of the woman I am –
don't just label me B.A.M.E.

It's not enough to crowd your spaces with people who
    look like me,
while the high places are filled with people who look
    like you.
Where is the representation at the top of this pyramid?
No space?
Let's change the shape.
Make a place for difference in the boardrooms and in
    the directors' chairs.
When there's representation where decision makers are
That's when change will truly start.

Do I look like 'another angry Black woman'?

Don't mistake my passion and unyielding fight against
    racism,
ableism, sexism, bigotry, exclusion,
and inaccessibility, for something as simple as anger.
I have something far more powerful.
I have action. I have passion. I have fight. I have
    resolve.
You wish I was angry.
Then, you could dismiss me.
Could pretend this is just a speech of abuse
instead, see, that this is me
shining a light on all that continues to go on in this
    sector that I love.

Silence doesn't equal peace.
Silence is loud and active.

If you're not actively a part of the solution then you're
   adding to the problem.

The sector I see
isn't afraid of difference and change.
It's fuelled by diversity.
It seeks to engage all instead of the few
and values every person for their individual identity.

And I will not stop until the sector I love becomes all
   that it should be.
So, take down your barriers –
I'm well within reach.
There is room for me, and you.

What Am I Building?

What am I hoping to step into and leave behind?

What am I building? What will I leave behind for Young
Lowe, for the world?
For Young Lowe, I hope to leave him with the courage
to be his full self, to be empowered in who he is and
what he is passionate about and to love the world
enough to seek empowerment for others.
For Wales, I hope to see a generation of empowered,
confident, connected Black women who courageously
innovate their work and bring others along with them. I
hope to rebalance inequity, teach others the importance
of and skill to integrate access in all of their work.
I hope to be remembered for those who I brought along

and the brilliant work they have accomplished.
I hope to be remembered as a woman who lived not
fearlessly but with courage and freedom. And I hope all
I've done to be only the beginning of all that's to come.

FROM PROHIBITION TO PROMOTION

By Norena Shopland

The Government of Wales Act 1998 resulted in the formation of the National Assembly for Wales, with devolved powers such as those previously held by the Secretary of State for Wales, and at least twenty national institutions including education and learning, and the Welsh Language. The legislation 'included a number of core values, including a commitment to equality, sustainable development, partnership working and parity of treatment for both the Welsh and English languages.'[1]

Yet inequalities for lesbian, gay, bisexual and trans (LGBT) people were retained, particularly in reference to Section 28. This legislation, prohibiting the 'promotion of homosexuality' (and by extension all other sexual orientations and gender identities) by local authorities, was still in place particularly in areas of education and learning, where bullying was rife, and the heritage sector had no representation of LGBT people. In the fifteen years this statute was on the books, there was not a single prosecution under Section 28, due partly to vague and ill-defined terms used such as 'promotion' and 'pretend families' that would have kept lawyers rich for years as they battled the government for definitive definitions.

---

[1] Senedd Cymru/Welsh Parliament, *History of devolution*, published 7 December 2020, last updated 7 October 2021. Available online.

However, more than anything it was recognised for what it was: government-sanctioned prejudice.

This is not to say people, including those in Wales, were inactive; there was opposition. In the year after devolution, Cardiff County Council followed an announcement by the Scottish Executive to scrap the controversial law. Cardiff Councillor Jane Reece received unanimous backing for her motion putting pressure on the Welsh Government to follow Scotland's lead, and in her speech described the stigmatisation that lesbians and gay men suffered and the ways in which the legislation hindered the provision of comprehensive educational, social and welfare services. Councillor Nigel Howells described Section 28 as 'an abhorrent piece of legislation' that 'provides a shield for homophobic bullying in schools, prevents education and was a bigots charter which legitimises discrimination against an easily demonised section of society.'[2] The UK Government indicated it might lift the ban in England and Wales but they would not do so for another three years.

Two years after devolution, in 2000, Education Secretary Rosemary Butler commissioned a review of how sex education was taught in Wales,[3] independent of whether Section 28 would be repealed. This was attacked by Tory Assembly Member (AM) for Monmouthshire, David Davies who produced an exhibition of literature at the Senedd of 'explicit material' that would, he claimed,

---

[2] BBC, 'UK: Wales, Council supports lifting 'gay lessons' ban,' 30 October 1999.

[3] *South Wales Argus*, 'Sex Education Review Ordered', 16 March 2000.

be available in schools if the clause was repealed; a move warmly supported by Tory party leader William Hague.[4] Labour AM, Val Field, condemned Davies' campaign as 'inflammatory and irresponsible' saying: 'It is fundamentally dishonest to claim to want understanding and a reasoned debate but then to openly appeal to base prejudice.' Much of the objections raised by Davies and others was the erroneous concept of 'promoting' homosexuality to children and that they alone were trying to keep young people safe. While they condemned bullying and urged teachers to tackle such harassment, it remained a contradiction that tackling bullying was by definition 'promoting' homosexuality. In addition, the 'explicit material' Davies featured had not been included in schools and this deliberate manipulation of misinformation lead to Davies becoming the first AM to be subjected to an investigation over standards of conduct and censured for his behaviour.

Davies continues to hold anti-LGBTQ+ (queer plus other sexual orientations and gender diversities) views, anti-equal marriage and anti-trans views yet he is now Secretary of State for Wales. How are we in a situation where someone with known prejudices is selected to represent all people of Wales? We need people in our government who will do all they can to uphold equality, not actively tear it down.

Davies and others like him did not consider the wider implications of Section 28, as due to its prohibitions libraries, museums and archives did not collect and are

---

[4] *South Wales Echo*, 'Attack on Section 28 display', 4 April 2000.

only now playing catch-up and it remains true that there is hardly any permanent representations of diverse sexual orientation or gender identity on public galleries in Wales. And there are deeper issues.

Most historic and contemporary narratives are male dominated and the lack of female representation is worrying. Take for example, Wikipedia, the largest online encyclopaedia in the world boasting nearly two million biographies – mainly of men.

In 2014, only 15.53% of Wikipedia's English language biographies were about women. [5] By 2022, through the efforts of the specially formed Women in Red project, this had risen to 19.31% meaning of Wikipedia's 1,911,715 biographies, 370,412 are about women; and, at the time of writing, it has reached 19.76%, an increase of only 0.2% in eight months.[6] Furthermore, the rate of uploading has decreased from, on average, 70 entries a day in 2015, to 80 a day in 2020 during Covid lockdown, to 40 a day in 2023. It may be that after the initial Women in Red launch and lockdown, the uploading rate has decreased to a natural level – but if the lower rate remains it will be 100+ years to reach equality.

Similarly, in Wikipedia's *List of people with an entry on the Welsh Biography Online* there are 4,481 Welsh people listed, of which 181 are women, equating to just 4%. Of any given 100 individuals the highest for women is fourteen and most entries date to the late nineteenth/early

[5] Wikipedia:WikiProject Women in Red.
https://en.wikipedia.org/wiki/Wikipedia:WikiProject_Women_in_Red.

[6] Wikipedia:WikiProject Biography.
https://en.wikipedia.org/wiki/Wikipedia:WikiProject_Biography.

twentieth centuries. The online *Dictionary of Welsh Biography* boasts some 5,000 concise biographical articles in Welsh and English with no indications of how many women there are compared to men. The administrators have admitted there are 'very few' and in 2024 received funding to improve this.[7]

These figures and other diversities are important because we live in a country where women's achievements are not recorded anywhere near to that of men. This has a knock-on effect in that diverse women are even less represented and the history of ethnic minority, disabled, lesbian, bisexual, trans and other diversities are not being celebrated.

Just as the National Assembly for Wales was being formed in 1999, the current First Minister, Mark Drakeford, co-authored a paper with Jonathan Scourfield of Cardiff University entitled, *Boys from Nowhere: Finding Welsh Men and Putting them in their Place*. In this, Scourfield and Drakeford looked at masculinity in Welsh men, but acknowledged the 'growing body of feminist literature on Women in Wales' developed to tell the 'hidden stories of Welsh women.' However, by studying men, they argued, it aided women because, 'if we accept the mainstream feminist premise that some men have disproportionate power in our society, then this power can only be fully understood by studying men.'[8]

However, it is this studying of men that skews the study

---

[7] Dictionary of Welsh Biography, 'Introducing the Diversity Project of the Dictionary of Welsh Biography,' DWB website. (https://biography.wales/amrywedd).

[8] Jonathan Scourfield and Mark Drakeford, 'Boys from Nowhere,' *Contemporary Wales*, Vol. 12, (1999), p. 3-17.

of women. Take, for example, the concept that due to the power exercised by men, throughout history women were for the most part restricted in their movements and ambitions. Yet this is not strictly true, as shown in my book *A History of Women in Men's Clothes,*[9] that relates extensive stories throughout the UK, and the world, of women who would put on 'male attire' for diverse reasons – to visit a sick aunty down the road when there was nobody to accompany her, to become explorers, sailors or soldiers, navvies, or simply to avail themselves of the much higher wages men enjoyed. Or, for those we might today recognise as lesbian and trans, who were able to live a more open life. Or of sex workers in Cardiff docks and elsewhere who cross-dressed as men to attract homosexual males, as being caught with a woman who looked like a man only incurred a fine, while being caught with a man could incur long years in jail and a ruined life.

In these cases, male power is represented as a pinnacle which women aspired to and the writings of society, mainly by men, presented the stories as understandable that the dear little things were of course jealous of male power. However, if we study the women, not the men, we see how tenuous that power really is if it can so easily be turned on its head. This approach to women's history through men can leave so much hidden.

In 2021, I approached Ceri Thompson, curator at the Big Pit Museum, about an exhibition on the myriad women working on the pit banks of coal mines during the

---

[9] Shopland, Norena, *A History of Women in Men's Clothes*, Pen and Sword Books, 2021.

nineteenth and early twentieth century. I had come across them in my work on cross-working women – many had defied laws banning women in mines and worked as men. Initially, there was concern about there being sufficient amount of information to support such an exhibition. So having done the research, it became clear there was more than enough data and fascinating stories of women's struggles in the coal world. For nearly 100 years these tenacious women fought to keep their jobs against men who wanted them out.

The subsequent exhibition by Thompson and myself remained in Big Pit for a year before being transferred to Swansea Waterfront, where it remained until March 2023 and is now available for other Welsh heritage bodies to borrow. Despite this, there is still no permanent representation of women working in coal at the Big Pit and women's supportive roles, as secretaries, nurses and canteen workers, are the only way of viewing women in an almost all-male museum. The only way to record and celebrate these women is through a book: *Women in Welsh Coal Mining: Tip Girls at Work in a Men's World* (Pen and Sword Books, 2023). Hopefully, some day in the future all heritage sectors covering Welsh mining will include women who actually worked with the coal, not just supported the men who did so.

One of the reasons why women working at mines and other highly laborious jobs were disapproved of was their perceived masculinity. Even though many did not cross-dress, they were seen as almost like men because they did 'men's jobs' and they did not look like society's expectations of what a woman was supposed to look like. This whole study of negativity towards perceived masculinity has a troubling history.

Marged uch Evans (1696–1793), a woman who lived in Snowdonia, entered the historical record purely because of her masculinity, becoming a tourist attraction in her own time and about whom several stories were later invented to illustrate her physical strength. Yet a children's book published in 2010, *Merched Cymru 2: Marged Arwres Eryri*, by Siân Lewis and with illustrations by Giles Greenfield, has pictures of Marged as a wasp-waisted, pretty woman. No descriptions of Marged survive, but given her laborious life – much of it working outside – which included rowing iron ore across the lakes of Llyn Padarn and Llyn Peris, surely she would be more swarthy and solid-looking like many photographs of rural Welsh women?

Instead, we have images in the book of a slight, pretty woman who in one picture is rowing a boat-load of copper ore across a lake. Similarly, *Cyfres Menywod Cymru: Cranogwen* (Gomer, 2011) by Elin Meek covers the life of Sarah Jane Rees, more popularly known by her bardic name Cranogwen (1839–1916), who went to sea with her father as a young woman and who became a master mariner. Again, a woman doing laborious work is presented as a wasp-waisted, pretty woman. For whom are these images intended, the male gaze? LGBTQ+ young people are bullied in higher numbers than the general population for not conforming to heteronormative narratives and girls who are not societally endorsed 'pretty' are also bullied for their appearance. So, is representing Marged and Cranogwen in this way not only doing these two individuals a disservice, but also letting down young people? We know women are bullied unmercifully on social media over their appearance and not their achievements, and these kinds of publications do nothing to address that. In addition, neither book includes details about the women's same-sex relationships, so young lesbians are deprived of positive narratives. Hopefully, in the future, these missed opportunities will be addressed and children supplied with images more representative of real life rather than the dolly-bird image and the sexually neutral narrative.

Both the books mentioned above are in Welsh, and devolution put the responsibility for the language with the Welsh government, but here too are gaps. Welsh language terminology for sexual orientation and gender identity generally follows that of the English language; that there are more terms for men than for women but much of that is driven by the criminalisation of male-to-male sex and its subsequent decriminalisation. Female-to-female sex was never criminalised but was socially unacceptable. Current work by Luke Blaidd[10] in creating the first extensive Welsh-English dictionary of sexual orientation and gender identity has found that no lesbian terminology appears in a Welsh dictionary until 1973, over a hundred years later than in English. Even then, the term only appears on the English side of the dictionary, not the Welsh. Variations on

---

[10] Blaidd, Luke , 'Term Anniversaries- Vital Landmarks for Welsh LGBTQIA+ History,' LGBTQ Cymru, 4 April 2023.

Lesbiaid/Lesbiaidd/Lesbiaeth appear sporadically in dictionaries until included more extensively in the 1990s. However, in 2008, Webster's Welsh-English Thesaurus Dictionary Clawdd, ('Dyke') appears as the sole term for lesbian in Welsh. There still appears to be an inconsistency of inclusion for lesbian terms in these reference works and many attempts at inclusion may be misguided (e.g., using Clawdd instead of Lesbiaidd etc.). A similar situation exists in relation to transfeminine terminology, as Blaidd notes. 'Most publications simply use trawsryweddol and do not go into specifics. It may be worth noting that this may be contributing to the invisibility of trans women (and men) in Welsh.' For bisexuality, there is 'no terminology differentiating bisexual women and bisexual men.' Blaidd's dictionary 'may aid women in the future by helping to provide a clear, accessible guide to Welsh LGBTQ+ language which hopefully helps people to find the terminology they need, faster, to reclaim terms, as well as help people who identify partially or wholly as women to experiment with new pronouns. It is my hope that my dictionary can also be a home for newly coined terminology to help fill the gaps that exist – especially for lesbian and trans women, whose terminology has quite sizeable gaps.'[11]

It was precisely these gaps which inspired my work on research, recording and writing on Welsh LGBTQ+ history. I started in 2010, co-managing the first trans funded project in Wales, *Gender Fluidity*, providing information leaflets for service providers as advice and

---

[11] Luke Blaidd, personal email.

guidance on trans matters in Wales did not exist at this time. Copies can now be seen in Glamorgan Archives.[12]

At this time, heritage representation was poor. Amgueddfa Cymru was beginning to look at its collections but elsewhere there was little. In order to tackle this I applied for a Heritage Lottery Fund (now National Heritage Lottery Fund) and received a year's grant to start constructing a baseline for our history – at £49,000 it was the largest LGBTQ+ funded project in Wales and resulted in an exhibition, the first in Wales, and a timeline that has since been updated and published as *Welsh Pride* on the RCT Pride website as a free download.

The launch of Welsh Pride, the Welsh LGBTQ+ people, allies and events exhibition was supported by many leading people of the day and their speeches can be read in *Welsh Pride*. As Ceri Harris, Equality, Diversity and Inclusion Specialist in the NHS noted:

> It seems so strange, looking back to think why in Wales we waited so long to have a LGBT+ project to look at Welsh Pride, but that's because we now see LGBT+ history so widely discussed and celebrated.[13]

In order to further this research and writing on the history of sexual orientation and gender identity, I wrote *Forbidden Lives: LGBT stories from Wales* (Seren Books, 2017), the first completely historical book. One of my aims was to

---

[12] Glamorgan Archives, Casgliad Norena Shopland Collection, Med 1929-Rhag 2018 / Sep 1929-Dec 2018, reference D1227/14.

[13] Ceri Harris, *Welsh Pride*, 2021. https://www.rctpride.com/wp-content/uploads/2021/02/Welsh-Pride-MAGAZINE-download-3.pdf.

ensure that the stories included equal representation as so many 'LGBT' events were, and still are, dominated by 'gay' with less material on lesbians, bisexuals and trans people. This was not as straightforward a task as I had originally thought, as the information on women was greatly lacking and experiences in researching original material proved problematic with regard to terminology.

It was precisely this struggle with female terminology that led to a series of experiments and the development of a new glossary that looked not at what people are, but what they were doing – and the most common activity lesbian/bisexual/trans people were doing was cross-dressing. Once I had adopted this methodology it proved extremely successful and I went on to recover over 4,000 articles, many of which have never been published outside their original source. Having stopped gathering material due to the necessity of moving on to other areas of work, the collection is now lodged with the LGBTQ+ Archives at Bishopsgate Institute, where they are currently at work to make the files open access. Hopefully, this will not only see more inclusion in the history of females taking power for themselves, but see more stories of those from the past we would today regard as lesbian or trans.

This methodology resulted in an extensive terminology list, the beginnings of which were included in a research guide, *Queering Glamorgan*, published by Glamorgan Archives, funded by the Welsh Government, co-authored by Daryl Leeworthy and downloaded well over 2,000 times. Since publication, the guide has been included on many international sites as a free resource due to its unique approach to research – the free download can be found on the Research Guides page on the Glamorgan Archives website. This later developed into my book, *A Practical Guide to Searching LGBTQIA Historic Records* (Routledge, 2020), which is essentially a toolkit in research and has been extremely popular.

What developed from this work was a series of training in LGBTQ+ language and history for leading organisations in the heritage sector – such as Amgueddfa Cymru, among others – attempting to bridge the gaps created by Section 28 that currently exist. Even today, with the exception of Amgueddfa Cymru, no museum in Wales has a permanent representation of LGBTQ+ people in its galleries. Celebratory events happen but once those are over, down come the pop-up banners, pictures and artefacts for another year, a bit like the Christmas decorations.

To help tackle this the Welsh Government commissioned me in 2021/22 and 2023 to provide five-part training courses on LGBTQ+ Language and History for local libraries, museums and archives. Many diversities suffer from a discrimination of disinterest: unless you have staff members or volunteers who drive projects forward then exhibitions are often dominated by mainstream celebratory events and the odd pop-up appears during LGBTQ+ History Month, Black History Month, International Women's Day and the like. The training is designed to assist those working in the heritage sector to look in depth at what can be done to celebrate local communities. In the feedback, 94% of participants said they would recommend the course and the Welsh Government recommissioned it for 2023. This training is intended to complement their LGBTQ+ Action Plan that was closed for consultations in October 2021 but has yet to be published at the time of writing. In the overview for the Plan, the Welsh Government states they aim to 'create a society where LGBTQ+ people are safe to live and love authentically, openly and freely as themselves' and embedding diversity in the national curriculum. In 2022, compulsory relationships and sexuality lessons began in Wales for children aged three to sixteen under the Relationships and Sexuality Education (RSE) Code:

> Across the learning strands, curriculum content in RSE must be inclusive and reflect diversity. It must include learning that develops learners' awareness and understanding of different identities, views and values and a diversity of relationships, gender and sexuality, including LGBTQ+ lives.

As to be expected, there has been controversy over this and sexual education in general, and there are ongoing attempts to reverse the ruling.

The Welsh Government's LGBTQ+ Action Plan follows the Anti-Racist Action Plan, and heritage consultant Marian Gwyn notes:

> Wales is being watched – I've attended conferences and meetings with people from the other constituent countries of the UK, where people have expressed their

regret that their own governances are not promoting or supporting diversity in the same way as Wales (through policy and funding). Several have said that they are keeping an eye on what happens here to see how effective this move is. There's a long-burn on something like this, as you know, but what stood out to me is that it is known that Wales is trying something different. It's seen as being bold and that people don't know what the impact will be (neither do we). I've discussed this with a few people and they confirm similar conversations.[14]

Similarly, I am on the International Committee of LGBTQ+ History Months and Rodney Wilson, the founder of LGBTQ+ History Month in 1994, agrees Wales is somewhere to watch:

The International Committee on LGBTQ+ History Months, with thirty-two members representing twenty locations around the world, is happy to have Norena Shopland as a founding member and representative of Wales. We closely follow what the Welsh government is making possible through its extraordinary leadership on LGBTQ education, history, and archival work – truly setting a high standard toward which more countries, we hope, will aim.[15]

One of the outcomes of the training that was commissioned by the Welsh Government, is the development of county

---

[14] Marian Gwyn, personal email.

[15] Rodney Wilson, personal email.

timelines to encourage research into local stories and move away from mainstream narratives dominated by non-Welsh individuals, international celebrities and events. If we are aiming to encourage more local people, allies and events to be celebrated, it is necessary to supply a baseline to get started. So in February 2023, nine county timelines were launched, hosted by individual organisations or groups, with an appeal made to local communities to add to the data so that they are part of the management of history. The details will be hosted on LGBTQ Cymru, a website funded by Swansea University, and dedicated to the publication of all thing's Welsh history and free for everyone to use.

Similar training courses have been rolled out to those who were not included in the Government's catchment of local libraries, museums and archives, such as national organisations like the National Library of Wales, universities and others.

This increased training is a timely development, and coincides with recent developments: 2022 saw more Pride events in Wales than ever before with Powys, Llanelli, Abergavenny and others holding either inaugural events or the resurrection of long-dead ones. With a 'firm ambition to make Wales the most LGBTQ+ friendly nation in Europe' the Welsh Government and NHS Wales signed up to a 'Memorandum of Understanding' with the Coalition Against Conversion Therapy in 2022.'[16] The Welsh Gender Service (WGS) was first announced by

---

[16] Welsh Government, Press release, Survivors of 'conversion therapy' among expert group helping advise Welsh Government on actions to ban "abhorrent" practice in Wales, 17 January 2023. Available online.

Health Minister, Vaughan Gething AM, in 2017 and is now based at St David's in Cardiff with Local Gender Teams (LGT) in each health board.

Action Plans and supportive investments have circular benefits because, as the old saying goes, success breeds success. I had long believed the principles set out in *Queering Glamorgan* and *A Practical Guide to Searching LGBTQIA Historic Records* could be transferable to any other subject and so in late 2022, Rhian Diggins of Glamorgan Archives and I designed an ethnic minority research guide based on these templates. An application to the Anti-Racist Welsh Government grant was successful and the guide will see more data being added to Welsh history and help those wishing to research. Hopefully, we can then see a similar move to have ethnic minority timelines for every county. But why stop there? We can use these templates for anything and have a whole range of research guides and timelines for every diversity because, at the end of the day everyone has at least one diversity that, when added together, make up the whole of society.

For a small country, the positive activism and contributions by myriad people have resulted in many firsts led by Wales, too numerous to mention here but they are covered in the timelines. Of course, things are not perfect and there is still a lot of work to do, but in 1998 the newly devolved Welsh Government prohibited the acknowledgment of LGBTQ+ people in its schools and heritage organisations, and now twenty-five years later its promotion of inclusivity is unique throughout the world.

MAKING THE HEADLINES - WOMEN AND POLITICAL BROADCASTING IN WALES

By Cerith Mathias. A roundtable discussion with Elin Wyn, Jo Kiernan and Elliw Gwawr

The advent of devolution and the creation of the National Assembly for Wales, now the Senedd, not only dramatically changed the political landscape in Wales, but also the broadcast media landscape. An ecosystem of programmes and journalism teams sprang up to report on and scrutinise the work of the newly-minted institution in Cardiff Bay, with newsrooms and studios established in Ty Hywel, the Assembly's first home.

All three major broadcasters in Wales, BBC Wales, HTV Wales (now ITV Wales) and S4C, carried coverage of the new political proceedings, and with that came new opportunities as the demand for political content and an understanding of devolved politics increased. But what impact did this change have on the experiences and career paths of female journalists?

My own career as a political journalist runs almost parallel with the timeline of devolution. I joined BBC Wales in 2002, just three years after the first ever Assembly election. I've worked on and then gone on to produce much of the channel's political programming, including flagship shows *Dragon's Eye* and *The Wales Report*, election programmes and network debate

105

programmes. Now a freelance producer, I work across all three main broadcasters, most recently producing *Y Byd Yn Ei Le*, at ITV for S4C.

Throughout my time as a political producer I've had the privilege of working with and alongside many remarkable women, who have been and continue to be pioneers within the industry. To understand both the importance of devolution in the story of female journalists in Wales and the impact of those journalists on the nature of political reporting here, I spoke to three others who have held a prominent presence in political journalism in Wales over the past 25 years.

Elin Wyn was the first Editor of BBC Wales' Assembly newsroom and established the S4C2 channel, which broadcast live from the Assembly each week. Prior to devolution, she was a senior news producer. She is now retired.

Jo Kiernan was ITV Wales' first and, currently, only female Political Editor. After a long career in journalism, she went on to be a Special Advisor to Labour First Ministers Rhodri Morgan and Carwyn Jones.

Elliw Gwawr is a Political Correspondent for BBC Wales. She spent a decade as a correspondent for BBC Wales in Westminster and has recently returned to Wales and is based in the Senedd.

On a cold day at the end of the political term in December 2022, I sat down with Elin Wyn, Jo Kiernan and Elliw Gwawr over a coffee in the Oriel of the Senedd.

Cerith Mathias

We've all come together to talk about the role of women in political broadcasting in Wales since the establishment of devolution, how things developed and how they've changed over the years. It's always interesting to me, that whenever we look back at the milestones of devolution, it's the contributions of male politicians reported on by male journalists that are remembered, while the vast contributions of female politicians and female journalists are rarely noted. The overwhelming impression is that there were barely any women involved. Whereas we all know there were women there at every level.

Jo Kiernan

There were women everywhere.

Elin Wyn

The whole thing was women.

Elliw Gwawr

Elin Jones [the current Llywydd of the Senedd] has talked at length about the importance of those female politicians right at the beginning, people who were doing the hard work. They weren't in front of the cameras, they were getting the agreements in place. The women in the background. They don't ever get mentioned, because they don't write about it, they don't shout about it.

Jo Kiernan

It's really hard to believe it's been 25 years. When did you come into journalism?

Cerith Mathias

I joined the BBC in 2002 and in 2003 I started working on the BBC-produced S4C2 Channel, just before the second-ever Assembly election. Elin was the channel's Editor and my first boss at the BBC.

Elliw Gwawr

I started at the BBC in around 2005, 2006. I went to Westminster to work full time in 2012 and I've just moved back to Wales and back to reporting on the Senedd.

Elin Wyn

I finished at the BBC in 2006.

Jo Kiernan

I started at HTV as it was known then in 1990, but I didn't specialise in politics until the mid-nineties.

Cerith Mathias

Jo and Elin, right back at the beginning of devolution, you were both already well-established journalists, Jo on air and Elin as a producer. But there were really very few visible women covering politics. Is that something that changed after the referendum in 1997?

Jo Kiernan

I was a Political Correspondent, and then Political Editor and pre- the setting up of the Senedd, or Assembly as it was then, I was the only woman in the team. But that changed quite quickly afterwards to a gender-neutral team, and ITV should be commended for that really, because we had two weekly programmes going out covering what was happening in politics, with different takes and different ways of covering things, plus the news team, and they were very keen to ensure that there was gender balance. There were two female presenters of those programmes, and obviously then a mixed group covering the news and the items for those programmes. So it was quite remarkable really.

Cerith Mathias

When the Assembly was being established, there was a clear aim of being different to the culture of Westminster. Did the broadcasters react in a similar way? Was there a feeling of wanting to do things differently in the way that politics was covered and by whom?

Jo Kiernan

There were two of us covering politics at HTV in the pre-referendum days and really only one covering it full time, [former Political Editor] Max Perkins. So, when you're creating this new thing, you have a great office, the corner office up there on the fourth floor of Ty Hywel, right in the heart of things, with a studio built into the corner so you could react quickly to whatever was happening in the Assembly. Why wouldn't you try and have a gender-balanced team? Yes, it was a conscious decision. But I think it would have been very easy given that the bulk of people applying would have been men, for them to have taken the easy option.

Elin Wyn

My involvement was to do with setting up the S4C2 channel and also looking at the broadcasting set up here in the Assembly. Cath Allen ran BBC Wales' Political Unit in its entirety, but she'd also been running the Westminster operation, not on camera herself, behind the camera.

Cerith Mathias

So women were in some key roles as things were being set up. What about on air?

Jo Kiernan

I think certainly back then in 1997 and 1998, and then of course with the first election in 1999, it was fairly male dominated. It was pre-Bethan Rhys Roberts [BBC Newyddion anchor], Betsan Powys [BBC Wales Political Editor 2006-2013], Felicity Evans [BBC Wales Political Editor 2018-2023] having senior roles.

Elin Wyn

Rhuanedd Richards [now Director of BBC Wales] was with us on S4C2 a little later as well.

Elliw Gwawr

By the time I joined, there were definitely a lot of young, female political journalists. We were being given opportunities and as you say, Jo, there were lots of political programmes, so there were more opportunities and more jobs. A lot of the more senior jobs were still male-dominated at the time, but we were still given those opportunities. When I started on S4C2, I was given on-air roles. It gave us a good training ground.

Elin Wyn

When I started S4C2, I had three in a team and the first team was two women and one man.

Cerith Mathias

I wanted to ask you about that Elin, because I remember when I joined S4C2 there were a lot of visible women around. You were the Editor, and Rhuanedd Richards was the presenter who'd followed on from Esther Prytherch and Beti George.

Elin Wyn

I don't think I had any male presenters in the beginning on S4C2?

Cerith Mathias

No, that's right. Not until quite a few years later when we broadcast journalists started presenting it. I remember there being a lot of women in the team. And I've got to be honest it didn't really occur to me, and I don't know if you felt like this, Elliw. Even though politics is quite a male-dominated area, because there had been visible people on air, like you, Jo, coming to the Assembly studio to meet you for the first time, Elin, it didn't necessarily feel like I was going into somewhere that wasn't for me.

Jo Kiernan
That it was different from the newsroom.

Cerith Mathias
Yes, exactly. I just thought, yes, this is absolutely somewhere I should be and want to be.

Jo Kiernan
If the referendum had been lost, if this place hadn't been set up, well I was already on this track, but I think a lot of the women that we see on screen at the moment – more so in the BBC, I think because of the volume of staff – but if S4C2 and the like hadn't provided those opportunities, women would still only be doing general news.

Elin Wyn
Yes, not politics, not the specialist correspondent roles.

Elliw Gwawr
Everyone who now has a more senior job, be it as a correspondent in politics or the specialists, nearly all of us [at BBC Wales] have had that training ground in S4C2 or the political unit and those opportunities mean that

some of us have moved on to other specialisms. But you know, a lot of us are still in politics and have stayed in it. And as you say, if this place hadn't been set up, would we have had those opportunities in the first place?

Cerith Mathias

Yes, similarly from my point of view as a producer, those early opportunities were invaluable. Going from S4C2 to producing pretty much every BBC Wales political TV programme, every iteration of each one, and there have been many! Also doing that in the independent sector with The Wales Report, those opportunities certainly wouldn't have been available pre-devolution.

Elin Wyn

Yes, it's difficult trying to remember the names of all of them as they've changed over the years. Esther Prytherch [former BBC Wales journalist and first presenter of S4C2] made a programme, 'The Office' towards the end of '97, the beginning of '98, which was a fly-on-the-wall programme following the passage of the Government of Wales Act in the Welsh Office, and of course, they also followed the work of The National Assembly Advisory Group, NAG. There were a lot of women on it. Helen Mary Jones [former Plaid Cymru AM and MS] was on it, a very young Kirsty Williams [former leader of the Welsh Liberal Democrats] was on it. And of course the head of the civil service in the Welsh Office was Rachel Lomax. She was very influential in NAG and in the passage of the bill. From the start, they decided they were going to do things differently to Westminster, with family-friendly hours and the style of discussion. Also the fact that the political parties themselves had decided to adopt some kind of positive action to make sure that there were more women elected. And it did make a difference at the beginning, I think. Because in the whole institution, you were aware that there were more women around us as politicians.

Elliw Gwawr

It definitely makes a difference to the atmosphere, having worked in Westminster, where even now you can still be in a room where you're the only woman. Whereas here, it's much less likely to happen. It's about how people behave.

Jo Kiernan

Westminster felt to me, you can imagine in the nineties, like an old boys' club. And I hated some of the traditions, the pomp and ceremony, that just felt really archaic to me. It's really interesting, because I do remember, as a little aside, that as lots of women were elected in 1997, Labour brought in lots of new women and there were a handful – it wasn't more than that – who really struggled and subsequently didn't stand again. I've never had a conversation with a single woman member here who said that the atmosphere, the being away from home, the kind of difficulty of making relationships, had forced them to think about not standing again. It was just completely different at that time.

Elin Wyn

I remember a little later on in around 2005, before I finished at the BBC, The British Council had a big international conference in Cardiff on women in politics, because we had gender parity in the National Assembly at the time. They had delegates from all over the world. I remember I was doing a paper there on the representation of female politicians in the media. I'd done an analysis of how many women were seen on the screen; I analysed the BBC and ITV and of course, although we had 50/50 elected, the proportion of women politicians on screen was far, far lower. Mainly because of the roles they had – they weren't party leaders at the time.

Jo Kiernan

When Rhodri Morgan took over from Alun Michael, I think there was a really deliberate effort to have gender balance. You had Sue Essex in the finance portfolio and the likes of Edwina Hart and Jane Davidson. So actually, I would suspect that I was interviewing women probably more than men for a period.

Cerith Mathias

Do you think that having more female journalists both on air and off air has made a difference to how many women have been represented on air? Because anecdotally, I remember a very senior politician saying to me that back at the beginning a group of female politicians had come together to complain that a particular programme wasn't including women regularly, and they apparently were given short shrift.

Jo Kiernan

It was very blokey back then, with conversations had in pubs or snatched conversations in corridors. I don't think there was a conscious effort to behave or act differently because we were women. I think that maybe our mindset, our concept of fairness, I'd like to think is inherent in what we do.

Elliw Gwawr

I have to say even though like we said, that initially there were a lot more women, later on, I certainly felt at one period like a lone female in here. So later on, I think, after S4C2 finished [the channel ceased broadcasting in 2010] and toward the end of the 2000s, there were fewer [political] programmes, fewer opportunities.

Elin Wyn

Yes, there were big cutbacks at that time.

Elliw Gwawr

The political journalism team became smaller, and so did the number of women. I would go to briefings and I would be the only woman in the room. So things did change. And I think maybe that initial enthusiasm, the attempt to get more women, it wasn't sustained. It's vastly improved again, so it's come in waves.

Cerith Mathias

Did being the only woman in the room impact on how you behaved in any way, Elliw?

Elliw Gwawr

I think it does have an impact. I think you do try and become one of the lads, because, if you've got lots of blokes in a room, the atmosphere does change, the kind of things they talk about, the banter. I wouldn't do it now, but as a young journalist, I thought that's the way it was. I remember females coming in and they were quite intimidated by it all. And they wouldn't last long and that was worrying. I remember at one point thinking, you know, things need to change, we need to get more women here and they need to stick around.

Jo Kiernan

You see, I didn't find that at all. I never felt that I encountered any of that sexism. I genuinely encountered much more sexism later on in my career than I did as a journalist.

Cerith Mathias

Would you say that more women covering politics and more female politicians is key to changing that culture?

Elliw Gwawr

For years I just thought that that's how it was with politicians. You know, patronising you, flirting with you. For years, I just accepted it, I would just brush it off. But then when the whole 'Me Too' thing happened, it was like a light bulb moment and I realised; it's not on, you know.

Elin Wyn
Was that general behaviour as bad here as it was in Westminster? I mean, I experienced bits of it here, but not massively.

Elliw Gwawr
I experienced it here and in Westminster. Nothing seriously bad. I was patronised terribly by lots of men.

Elin Wyn
Oh, lots of patronising.

Elliw Gwawr
Things like, if you're with a cameraman or another male journalist who might even be junior to you, politicians talk to them and not you. That's happened here and in Westminster. I remember a politician here when I'd just started saying, 'So what do you do then, little girl?' I'm a journalist, thank you very much!

Cerith Mathias
I remember setting up for an interview here, and the interviewee making a beeline for the male cameraperson and turning to me and saying rather dismissively, 'Oh I'll have a coffee.' And I said, 'No I'm the producer – I'll be going through the interview with you.'

Jo Kiernan

I don't think that happened in the very early days, it's something that's crept up.

Elin Wyn

I think the whole behaviour of this place, how they behave in debates, has changed. All this banging desks and things like that. You never had that before. It's gotten to be more like the behaviour in Westminster. The referendum result was so close and they wanted to try to make proceedings more consensual in the beginning. They weren't as antagonistic as they are now, it's changed a lot.

Jo Kiernan

I think the other thing that changed, first of all when everything was in Ty Hywel, before the Senedd was built, because of the way it was set out everyone, members of the public, the journalists, the politicians had to walk through a public area to get to the chamber. That's absolutely different to now.

Elin Wyn

It made a difference, the politicians were more accessible. I've always thought that there are so many faults with the design of this building. It separates the politicians from the public. They don't have to have anything to do with the public if they don't want to.

Cerith Mathias

Speaking of the design of the building, it's made me think about women in key positions back then. When the Senedd was being built, before the building was open, I remember coming here with you, Elin, in your role in the BBC's Assembly newsroom, and you were choosing where the inject points [the broadcasting points] went in here. It's so important to remember that women were in those key decision-making roles back then.

Elliw Gwawr

It's so important, isn't it?

Elin Wyn

I represented the broadcasters on the new building project board. So we decided where to put the inject points, where to broadcast from to get the best view and so on. There was an issue about putting one there [points to the balcony above the coffee shop in the Oriel], because that wasn't supposed to be accessible to journalists.

Elliw Gwawr

I remember we broadcast CF99 [weekly political programme broadcast on S4C between 2007 and 2013] from up there, and you're right, the camera crews had to cable down to where we're sitting now. Whenever I'm up there now I immediately think of presenting CF99.

Cerith Mathias

Looking back, what are the decisions you made or the actions you took, specifically to do with women on-screen or behind the scenes, that you're most proud of? Equally, is there anything you would do differently now? Big question.

Jo Kiernan

With me, I think, it's not a lightning moment, it's just trying to nurture female colleagues and offer support and to try to show them that it's not all about personalities and conflict – and trying to get them interested in policy and just to get them talking to people.

Elin Wyn

I think with S4C2, I felt really strongly from the start that S4C2 was the nursery slopes for journalism. So giving a rounded training in everything: writing, presenting, producing, so that there would be more opportunities open as you progressed.

Elliw Gwawr

In those days, that was actually unique. These days, journalists are expected to be able to do everything – film, report, write, produce and those who go to CJS [Cardiff School of Journalism] and the like are taught that, but I had never done journalism before and I was thrown straight in and had to write, film and edit and sit in a TV gallery and press all the buttons. We had to present the programmes, absolutely everything. It was such a great training ground.

Cerith Mathias

For me, it's developing female contributors. As a producer, you have to go the extra mile because if I had a pound for every woman I've phoned who was at the top of their tree who said 'Oh, you might be better off speaking to my colleague,' who always turned out to be a more junior man, I'd be very rich! It can often be difficult to convince female contributors to take part, and once they do, I always make sure I follow up with them afterwards to encourage them to do it again. Obviously with news, you need to move quickly which is why it's so important to put the groundwork in.

Elliw Gwawr

Throughout my career I've tried to push for more women on air, be they contributors or journalists. And for me, I want to show that women can do politics. Simply, you know, that we do have an interest. It really riles me, this idea that women aren't interested in politics, that really gets my goat. That's why we need to have women on air, women contributors, women experts. And like you said, Cerith, it is harder, it's more work, but it's so important that we do it. Women can often have a different focus. Doing stories about sexual harassment and about misogyny, we're the ones pushing those stories and I wonder if they'd ever get it done if it weren't for the female journalists doing them.

Jo Kiernan

Sadly, I think that back in '97, there was a sense of

optimism, of change, and in a way I think we've gone backwards.

Elin Wyn

I think we've gone backwards.

Cerith Mathias

In what way, Jo?

Jo Kiernan

I think in terms of the number of women in senior positions, reporting politics – and that includes all the broadcasters. As Elliw said, there was a period when it was really poor; it's been a bit cyclical. I think too in the number of men in senior producing and decision-making roles, those people who are deciding the stories and getting them on air.

Elin Wyn

Because that's absolutely vital, getting women in those kinds of positions.

Jo Kiernan

I just think it feels that the optimism we all had at the turn of the century has not lived up to our expectations.

Cerith Mathias

What can be done to change that?

Elliw Gwawr

You need more women in important decision-making roles. More women on screen, more women making the decisions. But I do think the problem now is there are fewer and fewer opportunities. We have far fewer programmes covering politics than we did at the beginning.

Elin Wyn

It's about framing what politics is. You don't describe it as politics. You describe it as life.

Elliw Gwawr

Of course, it's about everyday life and we all need to remember that.

Jo Kiernan

Well, you struggle to find the political programmes, they're tucked away in the schedule. When you think, back in the beginning, tiny HTV had two weekly political programmes plus news, and you know, I was doing stuff every night on the news. Actually I think the biggest problem with the lack of outlets is the nursery slopes we were talking about earlier, and developing talent. Because it's very easy to pigeonhole women into general news when they're first starting.

Elin Wyn

Yes, things that are seen as softer.

Jo Kiernan

Sadly, I don't think an increase in outlets is ever going to happen. I think the days of lots of weekly programmes have gone. But then you know, there's a whole new creative sector with social media now, where lots of younger people get their news. I don't know the answer to this, but I'd be interested in how many women are involved in producing news content for social media outlets. We need to make sure that women are producing that content. If that's where young people are getting their news and politics from, then women need to be there.

Cerith Mathias

That brings us full circle really, back to where we started this conversation. When this place was new, having women in key positions was vital. The same is true as the Senedd and coverage of it develops on whichever platform. Perhaps this is a good point to finish with. It made me think, Elin, of what Dafydd Elis Thomas [former Presiding Officer] said when you left the BBC.

Elin Wyn

It was my leaving party and we were downstairs outside the chamber and Dafydd Elis Thomas was the official host. He gave a speech and he said, 'Well, Ron Davies may be the architect of devolution, but Elin Wyn was the midwife of the Assembly.' It was very funny.

DEVOLUTION, CLIMATE CHANGE, AND HOW WE COULD
LEARN A THING OR TWO FROM THE BEES

By Rae Howells

a Bee is not a Bee.
a Bee is only this:
a simple cell, embryo,
a single golden hair
which eBBs and falls unheeded.

she is not more.
not a self of her own, but noBody.

and the colony is also
endlessly self-making, carBon copying,
seeding and reseeding,
each Bee giving its small Body for this Body.

It is spring 2018 and in a corner of a Gower meadow, a common carder bumble bee forages in the hedge. Her buzz is soothing and song-like, a low, susurrating hum that zigzags with her as she meanders from flower to flower. Her fingertip-sized body is sturdy but slim, her abdomen banded with pale yellow and toffee brown and her thorax is a distinctive foxy orange. She's a queen, not long emerged from hibernation. Like every queen that's come before her, her task now is to make a nest of dried grass, round as a hurricane, in which to build a wax bowl and lay her eggs. This is how she gets her name, by combing and neatening a tangle of grass until she has sculpted it into a hollow ball, like a textiles worker carding wool. From this chamber, she will raise the next generation of common carder bumble bees.

Later in the summer I will find her nest, and she will become the subject of a poetry book[1]. For now, she and I are here together in this small corner of Gower, tending to our flowers. Tucked among the identikit fields of lush grazing an unlikely square is cut from the turf. Within it, rows of spiky Mediterranean plants are sprouting up in defiance of the Welsh rain and heavy soil. Lavender seedlings, not yet in bloom.

This is my lavender field. Until recently I was a journalist running a community newspaper in Port Talbot. But journalism is an unforgiving and underfunded industry, especially in Wales, and by 2017, after almost twenty years in the newsroom, I had become burnt out by the demands of the (mostly bad) news cycle. So I have disconnected myself from the frantic 'OMG what happened' of news, and am concerning myself with other timelines – the 'right now this moment' of tending this field, the 'what might be' of its future. And in a moment of what I will call optimism this new me coalesces around the idea of building a business from the land: I decide to become a lavender farmer on my native Gower.

Did devolution bring me here? A Welsh woman, Welsh speaker, a mother, a writer, a journalist, a journalism academic, an entrepreneur, and lately a bee sympathiser and a climate worrier. There's no simple answer to that, I think. But a better question might be this: Will devolution help me get where I want to go? Can it help us tackle the grave challenge we now face, a global climate catastrophe with many of its causes far beyond our jurisdiction?

By summer 2018 our first harvest is almost ready. The most important thing I have learned in my first year of farming lavender is that it grows much slower than a herculean Welsh weed.

I'm lucky that the Gower weather has been kind. Rain has been plentiful, but not too much. The sun has shone, but not scorched the plants. Unfortunately, the weeds enjoy this lovely weather too. I must battle gigantic, muscular docks, thistles, brambles and nettles and a marching army of grasses, intent on laying down an impenetrable thatch of roots. And I have never seen dandelions like these. They have plunged their talons deep into the soil. Removing them without breaking the root requires a lengthy, almost surgical, procedure.

It is while I am down low to the ground, parting the earth with my trowel to trace the thin white bones of yet another dandelion, that I first hear the rattlesnake sound of the carder bee's nest. Honestly, there is nothing as visceral and threatening as a hiss in grass. The first time I hear it, I brace myself for a snake's strike – one of

Gower's famous adders perhaps? When nothing comes and the sound dies away, I think myself lucky. Surely a trick of the wind in the foliage.

But now the queen is alert to my weeding hands – there's no going near without triggering the burglar alarm. Again and again when I stray too close, from the centre of her metre-square exclusion zone she furiously warns me to keep away. *Hissss!* There's no way this could be wind in leaves. I scan the weeds. Then from a hole somewhere, a carder bee takes to the air. Then another. It's no more than an eye-sized hole in a swirl of undergrowth, but finally I spy her fortress: a beautiful twist of yellow grass; a bee's fingerprint whorl on the field.

The common carder bee is sometimes said to be the UK's most common bumble bee. And yet her story is anything but common. Her ability to survive and ensure the ongoing survival of her species is remarkable, wonderful – and exists mostly outside the regard of us blundering humans. Take the fact that this queen would have been fertilised last year. Alone in a pocket of earth, she hibernated through the long south Wales winter of frosts and unrelenting rain, the sole guardian of her future colony.

Another of her talents is her ability to decide how many females and males to lay, deciding exactly how many future queens, fertile males and workers will be needed to secure the future of this colony and, more widely of course, the species itself.

When her eggs hatch they will take on specialist roles – nurses and foragers, queens and males – together making a colony. A bee colony works so closely together it is almost itself a creature, with an intelligence and an intent that goes beyond each individual bee. Every year this group of specialists works together to raise a new generation of queens and males, and then all of them, except the fertilised queens, will die, and the process will repeat.

You can understand, then, how vulnerable she might be. *A whole colony stored inside a single queen.* What if she is starved? Poisoned? Frozen? Parasitised? Gobbled up? Squashed by a boot? What if she doesn't make it?

I weed very carefully around her nest.

From here, on Gower's raised dragon back, farm fields roll away in every direction, a largely green desert that, these days, is often maintained just for the purpose of grazing horses.

Of course, cattle and sheep are farmed here too, and cereal and vegetable crops are also produced on Gower. There is an increasing trend towards diversification – alpacas, Christmas trees, pumpkins, wildflowers, cut flowers, flax, sunflowers, goats' cheese and honey are some examples of the more innovative ways land is being repurposed. Beyond the ridge lies Cefn Bryn, just one of the many ancient areas of common land that characterise Gower's distinctive landscape, criss-crossed by roads, grazed by livestock and providing rich mixed habitat for insects, birds, reptiles, amphibians and mammals.

But even here, in these almost sterile green horse fields, there can be life in the margins. We might not see bears or wolves, but in Wales, our amazon is at ground level: around your boots you can find a miniature jungle bursting with exotic beasts. There are grasshoppers, froghoppers, mining bees, ants, spiders, ladybirds, hoverflies, wasps, beetles, moths and butterflies.

My lavender patch is in a field shared with horses and was previously entirely grazed by horses. But now that I am varying the lawn with food plants, I have seen rare red-girdled mining bees taking advantage of the bare earth around my plants to dig their tunnels and lay their eggs, and an astonishingly large orb weaver spider with a luminous orange abdomen, threading her delicate web between the flower stalks. I have rescued a fat toad which had become trapped in the water butt.

There is wildlife here, if you pay attention at soil level, and to the rich tracery of hedgerows and scrublands between the pasture. Tune in to its frequency, and you find an ecosystem thrumming its clockwork. By the grace of its ticking, whirring, buzzing engine my lavender plants have matured and thrived and are sprouting up scores of long spikes, bursting with purple. The flower heads are fat with oil. They leave spiced and fragrant traces on my fingertips.

The world turns. By summer 2021, the lavender is growing well and the business is thriving, (surprisingly, considering there has been a global pandemic). We use the crop to make natural skincare and fragrance products presented in planet-friendly packaging, and we're stocked by almost twenty independent retailers across Wales. Putting the planet at the heart of our business has been a major asset, and also gives me a feeling of doing something tangible about the climate crisis. But more than that, owning and running a local business has enabled me to meet and nurture a network, a community of like-minded small business owners who are also building people- or planet-centred enterprises on Gower. We are a colony of specialists, stronger together, reliant on each other for survival.

These new eco businesses are essential in the current climate and nature crisis. Strong communities are the way forward, so we're told. The received wisdom is that only by working together, from the grassroots up, can we hope to change the direction of policy.

It has been widely reported in recent years that the world is entering a mass extinction phase. Apex species, which sit at the top of the food chain and have the power to shape both landscape and ecosystem – bears, wolves and lions, for example – are on global red lists and in extreme danger of extinction.

Their plight reflects the health of the rest of the

ecosystem. At the bottom of this complex, interconnected pyramid, is the humble invertebrate. But these critters are also in trouble. There is a global collapse in insect populations, as habitat loss, exposure to pesticides, human activity like light, noise and air pollution, and warming temperatures combine to take their toll – an 'insect apocalypse' that some scientists have said is the result of 'death by a thousand cuts'[2]. Without insects, there will be no plants (as many would not be fertilised to produce seed), no birds (as they would have no staple protein in their diets), no amphibians (ditto), no reptiles (ditto), and so on up the food chain, all the way to the biggest apex predator of them all – humans. As we lose diversity from our ecosystem, it will become harder and harder to grow crops to feed ourselves and our livestock.

Ecosystems are finely balanced, although they can take a fair battering before they fail. In the UK, we have been systematically 'de-wilding' the landscape for millennia to suit our own purposes, for agriculture, food production, industry, construction, transport and even leisure. And over the last few centuries, in particular since the industrial revolution, humans have become adept at changing the world to suit ourselves.

Our ingenuity in adapting our environment for our own needs is compounded by massive population growth. Ten thousand years ago, there were 1 million humans alive on Earth. Today, our numbers have expanded to 7.8 billion. And as our numbers have grown, we have taken up more and more room, deforesting, reshaping, building hedges and roads, moving waterways and mountains, building cities and factories, and pressing the land to produce ever more food in ever more efficient ways.

It has been many centuries since the last apex predators roamed Britain's wilds. These animals are also known as keystone species because of their unique landscape forming abilities. They do this by keeping grazing animals on the move through fear of predation, which in turn ensures areas are not over-grazed and thereby provides mixed habitats of woodlands, scrub and pasture to encourage a wide diversity of beneficial wildlife, giving them plentiful food sources and shelter.

But Britain's bears, wolves and lynx were long ago hunted or persecuted from existence. The last native brown bear was likely killed in the early medieval period, around 1,500 years ago;[3] the last Eurasian lynx probably died out 500-1,000 years ago due to hunting and habitat loss.[4] Wolves lasted longer – with some tales recounting how the last wolf was hunted and killed in Scotland as recently as 1680.[5]

So what is left? We might view the rolling hills, hedgerows and grazed pastures of the Welsh countryside as wild and unspoilt, but in reality there is very little left untouched by human hand or not influenced by human activity. What we see out of the car window on a day out in the countryside is not an idyllic natural scene, but a grazed green desert of compacted lawn resulting from widespread sheep grazing, devoid of nectar-rich wildflowers, the necessary food of insects. The result is what the conservation writer Benedict MacDonald calls 'the greatest wildlife silence of all'.[6]

In his book *Rebirding*, a manifesto for rewilding Britain for the benefit of birds in order to rebalance the ecosystem and establish an ecotourism-focused economy, MacDonald notes that livestock farming (predominantly sheep farming) occupies 88% of the land surface in Wales while up to 80% of its workforce's salaries are subsidised by Welsh Government.

Meanwhile livestock farming contributes only 0.7% of the nation's economy and employs a mere 1.9% of its population. He argues that these subsidies would be better used to incentivise farmers to diversify their grazing lands, re-establish mixed habitats or even stop sheep farming altogether in unproductive areas – in other words, for re-wilding. These habitats might instead be devoted to reintroduced species such as lynx or white-tailed eagles, which, he argues, would be a draw for visiting tourists. There is a precedent in Wales in the shape of the red kite. The red kite was once commonplace across the whole of Britain, but a combination of systematic persecution and habitat loss saw it teetering on the brink of extinction in the twentieth century. A 130-year long protection and reintroduction effort – the world's longest running conservation project – has seen its numbers go from a few breeding pairs in the Cambrian mountains to more than 10,000 birds across the UK.[7] Red kites are now a major attraction in mid-Wales, and though data is hard to come by, a similar red kite project in Scotland is credited with generating £8.2 million for its local economy,[8] so it seems a safe assumption that red kite tourism is also benefiting the economy in Wales.

There's no doubt it is an exciting prospect to speculate which 'charismatic' species Wales might host in future – MacDonald suggests lynx or white-tailed eagles could bring £20 million for the local economy, based on the level of tourism eagles have brought to the Isle of Mull. Nobody is yet talking about reintroducing the lynx on a Welsh sheep farm, certainly not anytime soon, but the direction of travel in Welsh environmental policy is towards a more nature-focused agricultural sector.

MacDonald acknowledges a transition away from sheep farming in favour of ecotourism would not be easy, nor without controversy. Sheep farming is not just a means of making a living in Wales. Farming contributes £1.7 billion to the Welsh economy, but it also underpins a culture, a community, and I would add, is a foundation stone of the Welsh language. As he says, 'Rural communities are the backbone of Wales. Far more than sheep, it is cohesion and common purpose that rural Welsh communities fear losing the most.'

But if devolution has shown a talent, I think it is the ability to work with the in-built strength of communities in Wales. Indeed, The Senedd, and the Welsh Government themselves, are built on those pillars of community, cohesion, collaboration and cross-pollination. Like our native bees, our best selves are revealed when we listen to each other and work together.

However, as we all know, talking the policy talk is easier than walking the walk. Welsh Government has certainly shown it can do the former.

Land use is a key part of the Welsh Government's strategy as it strives (by 2050) to meet a zero-carbon target. This is now enshrined in Welsh law, namely The Environment (Wales) Act of 2016, a tangible result of the UK's signature on the 2015 Paris Agreement, which saw 195 countries agree to take action to limit global warming to 2°C.

For some years, the Welsh Government has sought to achieve significant elements of this net zero target by reconfiguring land use to plant forestry, to protect or reinstate wet peatlands, and to convert less agriculturally productive areas for renewable energy.

In the past Welsh Government schemes have incentivised farmers to plant trees, hedgerows or pollinator-friendly plants through schemes such as Glastir, Tir Gofal and Tir Cynnal. There have been tangible results, including positive outcomes for woodland and hedgerow bird species,[9] although Tir Gofal's impact on priority species was called 'disappointing' in a 2013 assessment of its outcomes by Alan Davies, then-Minister for Rural Affairs and Food.[10]

Nevertheless, in common with many countries across Europe, the Welsh Government presses ahead with rural subsidies as a way to deliver on its climate change pledges, with a new Sustainable Farming Scheme set to be rolled out from 2025 (following several delays). The scheme requires farms to devote 10% of their land to tree cover, and a further 10% to wildlife-friendly habitat. Wales is lagging here: similar schemes are already underway in England and Scotland.[11]

It's not hard to understand why such schemes are attractive to governments. Agriculture is currently responsible for approximately 15% of greenhouse gas emissions across Wales,[12] but farmers provide a ready-made network of land stewards, already invested in the land they manage, and they represent boots on the ground in delivering tangible, lasting change, if they can be persuaded to put their shoulders to the wheel. But the opportunity to drive the issue forward in partnership with farmers risks being lost. While the new rural subsidy scheme undergoes consultation, its headline reforms have proved unpopular, as recent protests have demonstrated. Among their complaints, farmers object to giving up valuable arable or grazing land for growing inherently (they say) low-value trees, and worry that the scheme risks drowning them in paperwork. Indeed, other 'big ticket' policies like the 20mph limit have also been controversial with the Welsh public, and there seems a growing mis-step between policy and public opinion. If nothing else, the Welsh Government's polling, comms and PR could use some work.

Perhaps it's a good thing that the solution doesn't all rest on the shoulders of farmers. Climate policy is also targeted at transport (15% of emissions), business and industry (24%), energy (26%) and residental (10%) – in fact, across all the business of government.[13]

A trio of legislation, all passed at around the same time – the Environment (Wales) Act 2016, the Well-being of Future Generations (Wales) Act 2015 and the Planning (Wales) Act 2016 – has sought to go further than rural subsidies to create a joined-up legislative framework for sustainability in Wales, with the three acts intended to work in harmony across seven wellbeing targets including resilience, which encompasses biodiversity and environmental sustainability, as well as setting planning laws within a sustainability agenda, and enshrining those important zero carbon targets.

Within this way of thinking there seems to be an understanding by Welsh Government that we are facing two different (if interconnected) challenges under the umbrella of 'the climate crisis': i) global warming; and ii) a nature crisis. Global warming has global causes, requiring management of our carbon outputs – i.e. systematic change to the way we use power – as well as the planet's carbon absorption systems. This is a complex problem that requires humans to quit our addiction to fossil fuels, while also protecting forests and peatlands that either naturally store, or absorb, carbon from the atmosphere. The second problem is around ecosystem crash, and although ecosystems are complex and frequently interwoven, often it is localised pressure such as habitat loss (those pesky mown lawns) or pollution that causes animal populations to decline. If we remove those local pressures, then systems can often recover. Replicate and repeat this micro-restoration over and over, and wider trends emerge.

In its lawmaking, the devolved administration has set a tone. Policies like the plastic bag charge, the ground-breaking future generations act, banning single use plastics, the net zero commitment, encouraging workers to work from home, the refusal to build the Newport bypass for example, are all news headlines that have nailed certain colours to the mast of Welsh life, that have made clear that the climate is towards the top of the priority list. And so it's all to play for. Perhaps this atmosphere is creating fertile soil, a feeling of like-minded people all pulling in the same direction.

But so we come to that sticky second half of the phrase – the bit about 'walking the walk'. Big single department policies are one thing, but what happens when aims straddle departments, requiring change, coordination, cooperation? Or where cooperation might need to come from local and regional and national, and/or across big, unwieldy departments? This is where the cracks can show, because it's much more difficult to put things into practice in the real world, when – to stretch the analogy – all the various different types of bees, the bumble bees and miner bees and honey bees, have to come together and work with each other with sometimes limited resources.

I hope Welsh Government's ambitions can stand a real-life test. I have become involved in a local campaign to protest against a housing development on a small piece of Gower common land, known locally as West Cross Common.

It's a stunning, scrubby little place, bursting with bees and butterflies (you had me at bees), with rare food plants and scores of birds, reptiles, amphibians and mammals, from adders and polecats to bats and greenfinches. It has been joyously neglected and ignored for decades. It is boggy, overgrown, and dismissed by some locals as waste ground. But guess what? Neglect has made it wild. It is incredibly biodiverse, spilling over with rarities like devil's bit scabious, tormentil, bog asphodel and waxcap mushrooms. It is a type of lowland wet heath known officially as 'purple moorgrass and rush pasture', which is listed by Natural Resources Wales as a priority habitat with a target of 'no loss'.[14] If you go by the Welsh Government's climate policies on peat alone, there's no way it should be developed.

However West Cross Common (or Land North of Chestnut Avenue, as it is known on the planning application), situated as it is on the edge of the SSSI-designated Clyne Common and Gower's infamous Area of Outstanding Natural Beauty (AONB), also has the misfortune to be located on the rim of the existing settlement of West Cross. Welsh Government planning policy on sustainable 'placemaking' means that this land can be put forward as an 'exception' site, a slice of green belt that can be nibbled away for the purposes of affordable housing.[15] Planning permission has already been weighed and granted at local level by Swansea Council, with the promised affordability of the housing tipping the scale in its favour. However, as it is common land, the final decision rests with Welsh Government, which must be satisfied that the land's importance for such things as rights of commoners, biodiversity, amenity value for the local community or its carbon storing peat soil, can be outweighed by the provision of 56 affordable rented homes and 70 parking spaces.

This kind of dilemma forces us to confront a bigger question: What sort of Wales do we want? We are forced to make difficult decisions. Roads that are needed, but shouldn't be built. Speed limits that nobody is complaining about, but that ought to be lowered. Greenbelt housing developments to keep up with a dire shortage, but which shouldn't go here. Decisions that can feel limiting, inhuman, bonkers, and perhaps worst of all *fluffy*. But which ultimately take us towards a cleaner, safer, greener Wales. Each difficult choice is another brick in the wall, if we can only have the courage to keep building.

Wales is a small nation. We are 3 million people among a global population of 7.8 billion. We are just one bee. How can the Welsh Government hope to make a difference to global climate trends? Obviously it can't. Not alone, anyway. But our small nation can do two things. First, it can stand up and be counted; it can do its bit, clean up its own back yard – the grassroots, bottom-up approach. Second, it can join the wider effort, collaborate with other nations, as it has with the Paris Agreement – help achieve top-down, systematic change. A queen in the colony.

Even though it often feels hopeless, I'm glad *somebody* is trying to do something at national level. Sure, we can all do our bit, but it's much easier if the Government is doing some of the heavy lifting, and there seems frustratingly little being done from the UK centrally. From here it seems

Westminster is paralysed, a rabbit in the headlights of party political in-fighting, a spinning carousel of prime ministers, and a complicated tangle of post-Brexit and post-pandemic difficulties, in thrall to lobbyists, big media and big money.

While they fight over immigrants in small boats or hold Covid inquiries so we can all learn (surely blindingly obvious) lessons about government procurement methods, we're all over here in the real world, desperately hoping to avoid the worst of those terrifying climate science predictions, please.

At the beginning, when we first started growing lavender, we took a 'bare earth' approach, battling weeds, pulling them up, keeping the soil exposed, and uprooting any plants that took hold as they endangered our lavender crop. For the insects at our feet we might as well have been tearing up centuries-old redwoods, or the ancient trees of the Amazon rainforest.

Immediate problems became apparent. Soil eroded. Where we initially simply pulled up grasses to bare the earth, opportunistic (and much bigger) weeds quickly took hold. Where we could have trimmed or cut the grass and kept the soil securely in place, we were now battling enormous dandelions that competed for light and water with our lavender, and thistles that pierced our gloves and spiked our legs. We had made the land inhospitable to the plants and insects that seemed to keep it healthy, and made things harder for ourselves. We learned a valuable lesson.

We realised fairly quickly that it was in our direct interest to encourage this tiny soil-level Amazon to thrive. We are lucky that the lesson was so obvious. Not everybody will have such a direct and measurable connection between a thriving insect world and their own success. And many will actively hate insect pests and the damage they wreak to carefully sown crops, and be glad of their demise.

Either way, we are all tied to their fate.

Summer 2022. In my hands, I'm holding a poetry book, *The language of bees*. My poetry book. It tells the story of a dying common carder bumble bee. There are poems about lavender, about the catastrophic collapse of insect populations, about motherhood and miscarriage. Through writing the book I have come to appreciate how bees work together, not as individuals but as a colony, for the good of all – ideas I've tried to explore further in this essay.

Down on my patch the lavender is alive with hundreds of foraging bees, of many different species. I kneel in a row of purple and as I cut back the weeds, they drone around my head, bumping into me, probing in case I might be another flower. As I move along I disturb resting moths with drab camouflage, crane flies which jangle up and make off in a panic, grasshoppers that spring off in surprising directions. We have let the wildflowers grow nearby, so when the lavender is done there will be plenty of food left for them to eat.

As we know, climate change makes certain disasters much more likely. A localised flood, drought or fire on my lavender field could easily spell a quick end for the bees, and equally a quick end for my business. The nature crisis could bring a slower catastrophe: no worms and beetles would mean degraded soil health on my lavender patch; no bees and butterflies would leave the plants unpollinated, the flower stalks unable to develop seed. The business might manage for a while but surely would eventually fail. And anyway, who, honestly, would want to farm lavender if there were no bees humming among its stalks?

What works here, in this exact field, with its particular aspect, its weather patterns, its proximity to the sea and the way the wind blows across it, its soil condition, its microbes and fungi, its seed store, the insects and birds that live here – may not work on the farm next door, nor on the plot of land down the hill, never mind in other parts of Gower or Wales. I recognise of course that lavender is not native to Wales (yes, ironic after everything I've argued), though it has as long a history here as rabbits; definitely medieval and possibly Roman.[16/17] But as with any other crop, growing successfully here requires time and patience, to learn how to bend with the land's moods and tendencies, and not to strive in opposition to them, not to impose an outside will on a system that already has a culture of its own, but to take the time to listen and discover how it already works, and build from there.

I think this is how politics should work as well. It is why I voted for devolution, way back in 1997. It was only my second outing as a voter aged just twenty. I remember it well. My father and I stayed up until the early hours to hear the result. We took to our feet and danced around the room in celebration when the 'Yes!' came in.

The idea that we could govern ourselves, in our own language and in a way that responded to our own needs as a nation, was exhilarating. It brought democracy closer to us. Real change seemed possible. This is the same reason I loved and have advocated for journalism, and local news reporting in particular, and why I have written and spoken extensively about the necessity of local journalism to a healthy public sphere in Wales.[18/19/20] Having a politics that is able to exist in its own place, in close conversation with its people, is crucial. And it's why I think devolution is – at least in theory – a brilliant idea.

Whether it has always been successful is open to question (my father has been disappointed by the levels of bureaucracy and thinks not). It is a relatively young parliament. Mistakes are bound to have been made. But surely by its very proximity to its citizens the Welsh Senedd is much better able to serve the people of Wales than distant, out-of-touch Westminster ever was – or ever could be. Like my little field, localised solutions have the benefit of being much more closely tailored to the people they aim to help, and therefore have a better chance of success. And if not, at least the politicians are much closer and more accountable when we shout in their ears that things need to change.

I think of her, the single common carder bee queen, faithfully carrying her eggs through the winter, sculpting her wax bowl, tending her larvae until they are able to form the colony and lay down their store for next winter. If she dies, the whole colony is lost. Each and every queen is important. Each and every bee, every worker, every male, is crucial to the survival of the whole species. Each one needs access to a safe place to live and raise her young, a reliable food source, and a clean environment free of toxins.

If we can get our little piece of the world right, then that's got to be worth something. The Welsh Government must keep going with its green agenda, but it needs to move much more quickly. And be even bolder. It must make, and crucially *deliver*, policy that recognises that the future of Welsh people requires a healthy Welsh environment. It must put nature first. It must stop tinkering around the edges, and truly rewild large areas of the country. It must rethink the way we use land in Wales and put trust in farmers as stewards and guardians of their land, who have a vested interest in the health of the ecosystem – and reward them for their efforts.

And this is where we are. Summer's heat seems to have gone on longer this year, unseasonably so. My lavender is still putting up flower spikes in October. The plants need to be pruned before the frosts set in, but I don't cut it all back. The common carder queen is still visiting, taking her chance to feed before winter closes in. I will leave her some bright sprigs of purple, and hope to see her again in the spring.

References:

[1] Rae Howells, *The language of bees* (Parthian Books, 2022).

[2] 'Insect decline in the Anthropocene: Death by a thousand cuts', PNAS. January 11th, 2021. https://www.pnas.org/doi/10.1073/pnas.2023989118.

[3] Helen Briggs, 'Lost history of bears in Britain revealed', BBC News. July 4th, 2018. https://www.bbc.com/news/science-environment-44699233.

[4] 'Into the wild: Could lynx be reintroduced to Scotland?', BBC News. February 2nd, 2021. https://www.bbc.com/news/uk-scotland-highlands-islands-55857070.

[5] Adam Weymouth, 'Was this the last wolf of Britain?', the *Guardian*. July 21st, 2014. https://www.theguardian.com/science/animal-magic/2014/jul/21/last-wolf.

[6] Benedict MacDonald, *Rebirding* (Pelagic Publishing, 2019).

[7] A triumph for conservation https://www.rspb.org.uk/our-work/our-success-stories/a-triumph-for-conservation/.

[8] Tourists spend £8.2 million in Dumfries and Galloway after travelling to see red kites https://www.rspb.org.uk/about-the-rspb/about-us/media-centre/press-releases/tourists-spend-8.2m-in-dumfries-and-galloway-after-travelling-to-see-red-kites/.

[9] Dadam and Siriwardena, 'Agri-environment effects on birds in Wales', *Agriculture, Ecosystems and Environment, Volume 284.* November 15th, 2019. https://www.sciencedirect.com/science/article/abs/pii/S0167880919302038.

[10] Davies, 2013, Written Statement – Outcomes of Tir Cynnal and Tir Gofal Monitoring and Evaluation Programme, https://www.bbc.com/news/uk-wales-58638544

[11] BBC News, 'Welsh farm subsidy changes delayed again to 2025' https://www.bbc.com/news/uk-wales-58638544.

[12] 2020 Wales Greenhouse Gas Emissions https://www.gov.wales/sites/default/files/publications/2022-12/greenhouse-gas-emissions-infographic-2020.pdf.

[13] Wellbeing of Wales report, 2023 https://www.gov.wales/wellbeing-wales-2023-globally-responsible-wales-html#:~:text=Most%20of%20the%20increase%20in,the%202019%20pre%2Dpandemic%20level.

[14] Wildlife Sites Guidance Wales: A Guide to Develop Local Wildlife Systems in Wales (2008)

[15] Planning Policy Wales, Edition 11, 2021 https://www.gov.wales/sites/default/files/publications/2021-02/planning-policy-wales-edition-11_0.pdf.

[16] Lavender history https://www.hitchinlavender.com/lavender-history/#:~:text=It%20was%20as%20early%20as,growing%20areas%20in%20the%20country.

[17] Rabbits arrived in Britain 1,000 years earlier than thought https://news.sky.com/story/rabbits-arrived-in-britain-1-000-years-earlier-than-thought-11696820#:~:text=A%20fragment%20of%20bone%20reveals,shores%2C%20possibly%20as%20exotic%20pets.&text=Rabbits%20arrived%20in%20Britain%201%2C000%20years%20earlier%20than%20previously%20thought,in%20West%20Sussex%20has%20revealed.

[18] Journey to the centre of a news black hole, Rachel Howells https://orca.cardiff.ac.uk/id/eprint/87313/

[19] *The Welsh Way: Essays on Neoliberalism and Devolution*, Parthian 2021

[20] *Hyperlocal News*, Routledge, 2018

TANGLED THOUGHTS FROM A MIGRANT MOTHER*

By Sophie Buchaillard

In April 2022, I was sitting at our kitchen table in Penarth, watching my then eleven-year-old son eat his breakfast cereal. The radio was reporting on the lack of progress faced by thousands of Ukrainian mothers and children seeking refuge in the UK, stories punctuated by the crunching sound of my boy, absorbed in his morning routine. 'How do you think you'd feel about being forced to leave your home like that?' I asked him. He looked up from the bowl and stared at the radio for a moment. 'Very sad. I'd be very sad to leave everything and everyone I know behind.' I nodded. 'Of course,' he added, 'it would be easy for you.' A little taken aback, I asked him what he meant. 'Well, moving here was easy for you.' In his mind, the story was a clear journey from A to B. He could appreciate the sense of loss associated with leaving a familiar environment behind, a feeling every child must be able to relate to; and he could imagine the journey itself: traversing Europe, escaping danger, something worthy of an adventure book. And like every good story, it had to have a happy ending: once *they'd* arrived, all would be well. *They* would be like *we* were, a mother and child sat at a kitchen table, eating breakfast.

---

* Part of this essay was first published as two short essays in *Wales Arts Review* (April 2022) and in *The Agenda*, (Institute of Welsh Affairs Agenda, August 2022).

Moving is easy for you: my own migration story was banal, so understated in fact I probably never named it as such. I spoke to my son of movement: a simple transfer from one city to another, Paris to Cardiff, no more eventful than relocating from Manchester. I spoke of opportunity: a bonus post-graduation-year-abroad with a nameless boyfriend. It amused him to hear that, a student in my twenties, I had never even heard of Wales. I was being led, on an organised trip designed to provide a flavour of exoticism, a sort of extended visit, to bolster an otherwise blank CV. A way to delay adulthood. I had explained that it was the era of free-movement, a given my generation couldn't imagine would become a dot on history's unravelling timeline. He knew I came from Paris, via Bordeaux, and a bunch of other places. I came to a morsel of land, west of the British Isles, a place like any other. I was young, unattached, carefree. One job offer led to another. I met someone, fell in and out of love a couple of times. There was no reason to go back. No obstacle for me to stay. A simple story from A to B, then. One in which I had silenced all the steps in between.

At the start of the millennium, a group of eleven prominent French travel writers attempted to re-define travel literature. They wrote of wandering-literature, of global literature. Strangely, in their re-definition, they provided a list of those whose story they felt couldn't be called travel. The experience of migration, they wrote, could not be captured by travel literature since its protagonist had been thrown into movement, often brutally. Migration to them, implied an unvoluntary journey, and by extension a certain lack of agency. From their perspective, all migrants were amalgamated with those seeking refuge, ignoring with one swoop many other motivations to travel. These men (all eleven were indeed privileged white men) are not alone in this perception. The result is that migrants are discouraged from telling their story, which in turn perpetuates stereotypes about who the migrants are. This narrow perception draws fixed lines between migration and travel, the latter associated with adventures and tourism. A journey there and back, from a fixed vantage point, opposed to, well, something else.

A few weeks into the war in Ukraine, television screens had been filled with images of dishevelled women and children crowding on train platforms in a country not so distant from our own. At the other end of their journey stood Poland and Germany, turned overnight into large-scale refugee hubs from where the rest of Europe operated pop-up schemes to welcome their share of refugees in an act of well publicised solidarity. The news propagated comparison with the experience of World War Two. In Penarth where I live, houses were draped in blue and yellow, some of the same houses that had carried placards urging to vote for Brexit only a few months before. Listening to the radio, I was reminded that when migrants are depicted as anonymous, homogeneous masses by an external eye, the story ends at the shore of the *host* country.

The story that is never aired is that even in the case of voluntary migrants, moving is often a push, brought on by external circumstances; a reaction to ghosts we leave behind, disguised as free will. To me, moving is a euphemism I continue to use to describe a journey, to pretend my position is fluid. The word 'migration' too heavy with baggage. I don't speak of the assessment meeting to gain National Insurance. Of the way the administrative officer addressed me in that tiny grey room, of his innuendos, his wandering hands. I gloss over what happened after the student year, when my residency status excluded me from accessing state support, when I lost my job, my house, when I slept on park benches for months. I silence the confusion I felt, and continue to feel, faced with a myriad of situations for which I lack the proper context, reminded I am an outsider, over and over again. I smother the fury I felt when, confronting the midwife who had carried out tests I'd declined, she replied that 'You foreigners don't know what's best for your babies.' I hide the sadness when my son refuses to learn French, knowing we will never share large pieces of who I am. I dream in a language neither my husband nor my son speaks, as if this side of me was condemned to remaining in a locked-away suitcase whilst I move in translation, always.

In year seven my son studied migration in geography class. On the first page of his school book I found a definition neatly traced in pencil. Migration: movement from one country, place or locality to another, *in search of a better life*. What the neat definition obfuscates is the less savoury narrative of daily life, played out in administrative offices, GP surgeries, schools, shopping centres and playgrounds; in the slightly raised voice, the slowing down of speech, and the 'Where do you come from?', repeated, like a litany, over and over again. It is the slow and inexorable gap that will grow between a mother filled with another language, another place; and a child, malleable, porous like a sponge, made into a different culture. If moving was simply the capacity to change place, to better our lives, then it *would* be easy. But migration is not an event. It is a lifelong sentence, governed by strong contradictions. In most people's mind, it is a one-way trip. A quest for betterment.

Yet the implications are uncomfortable, reminiscent of hierarchies of cultures and colonial era. What migration is, fundamentally, is a journey between cultures; one which can be linear, seasonal or circular. Beyond that, people's individual circumstances are vastly different, their motivations diverse, their expectations broad. Migration has the power to enrich us by gifting new perspectives on the world. Yet equally it can cast us adrift. Leave us untethered as the culture we left behind fades in the distance, whilst the new one renders us unwelcome. Migrating is to experience another culture intimately, beyond the image it wished to project of itself. Victor Segalen wrote about journeying between cultures: the one we carry with us, the other we are confronted with. And it is true that the eye of the migrant casts a perspective that amplifies the good and the bad. One that can reflect a familiar society back to us, from a multitude of dissonant perspectives.

By October 2022, the media are full of a new catchphrase: *the migrant crisis*. Except it is not clear whose crisis they are referring to. *The Today Programme* is reporting on the Manston Processing Centre, a gateway to the system set up to welcome and register those seeking asylum in the UK. Following a visit, the Independent Inspector of Borders described the conditions in the centre as 'wretched'. We learn that 4,000 men, women and children have been held there, some for weeks. We hear that the Centre was only designed to hold up to 1,500 people, for a few hours. In response, the Home Secretary speaks of an 'invasion'. Alone in the kitchen, I question the invisible voice of the radio presenter. 'Have we learnt nothing from World War Two?' A few weeks on, the numbers will have dissipated, people scattered in hotels up and down the country, out of sight, waiting to be processed, probably waiting for years, quantified only by volume.

The buzzer of the intercom rings. My son is home from school. Switching to a music channel, I ask how his geography homework is going whilst fixing him a snack. The teacher asked him to interview a family member about what it means to be British. He shrugs. 'Well go on, what did Dad say?' He wriggles on his stool. 'That he couldn't help me because he is Welsh, not British.' I smile, thinking of the many times I corrected my mother when she used *England* as the generic term to describe where I live. To the rest of the world, English and British are interchangeable, Wales often glazed over. The distinction matters to a Welsh person. To be Welsh is to be attached to those details. So as fate would have it, I will be the one articulating for my son what it means to be British. But what to tell him? That I got to swear allegiance to the Queen and her descendants in a ceremony that took place in a dusty office in Barry in front of two strangers? That each step in the process was designed to make me feel like a suspicious outsider? That the result was a passport that holds no more power than the one I already had? The identity that matters, the one that makes voices rise in the rugby stadium, eludes me. 'Something amazing happened today,' he interrupts me. 'A supply teacher pronounced my name right first time.' The label of migration, spilling onto my son. I recall that day, halfway through primary school, when I realised that he didn't know how to pronounce his last name because well-meaning teachers had butchered it over and over again. *Sorry, but I am so bad at foreign languages.* Thinking back, when my son was smaller and he got invited to a costume party, I would always dress him in a stripy top and a fake moustache. It was easy. That word again. Me secretly glad that through the cliché we grew a little closer. Now I worry what impact this might have had on my son's sense of identity. *Britishness.* I don't know what to say about it. In the end, I describe the formalities, convey the non-event. Suddenly what I want more than anything is to normalise, to reassure.

At the first parents' evening in secondary school, we were invited to an information session about the new Curriculum for Wales, a ninety-minute presentation from a Deputy Head Teacher I had never met before. She was keen to share her enthusiasm for this new programme. 'Developed in Wales over a seven-year period, it aims to prepare the next generation for the jobs and challenges of the future,' she announced, praising the way subjects would be integrated around cross-cutting themes. 'If you take migration for example,' she said, 'your children will be studying the history of migration in one class, the migration patterns in geography, and because of the commitment to diversity and inclusion, they will learn that those people live amongst them, in our community.' *Those people. Our community.* I shuddered. Of course, she didn't mean anything by it, I told myself, for the millionth time.

In the world in which my son is growing up, words are increasingly weaponised. The National and Borders Act created a two-tier asylum system: people entering the UK via irregular means now risk being criminalised and deprived of the rights defined in the 1951 Refugee Convention. In response, the Welsh Government decried the *hostile environment policy*. Thanks to a cross-party consensus, Wales vowed to mitigate its effects on refugees and people seeking asylum. The result is a vision of Wales as a Nation of Sanctuary, underpinned by a detailed action plan which levers devolved powers to seek rapid integration. I am glad to be living in a country that is able to articulate such laudable aspirations. At the same time, I have not forgotten that not so long ago, a majority of the population here voted for Brexit, a dissonant reality that is hard to reconcile.

The day of the Brexit referendum, my son's primary school rang. A teacher had mentioned the results in class, and my son had gotten distressed, thinking someone was going to come and take me away. He was five years old. I left work, collected him, and we sat together on a bench

in Roath Park looking at the Canada geese taking flight.
'It's ok,' I whispered in his ear, wondering if I was telling
the truth. The next day, I started the paperwork to obtain
British Citizenship.

In 2023, I reached a milestone of sorts. I have lived in
Wales longer than in France. I didn't celebrate. In fact, I
don't think I mentioned this to anyone, because I realised
most people wouldn't care. Only my friends with a lived
experience of being between cultures themselves might
appreciate the conflicting emotions that come with the
realisation I have been *other* the majority of my adult life.
A mother, I wonder about the fate of children like mine,
children whose parents are hyphenated – Franco-British –

White-Other

A little boy whose second language is Welsh, but whose
mother tongue is ambiguous, leaving gaps
                       in which others will pour their
                           ill-guided interpretations.

  I worry about the effects of
    the hostile-environment
      the broken environment
        the polarisation of this world.
          I fear that being well-meaning is no longer
        enough.

Perception is everything. Crossing the Severn bridge, my
son always cheers at the Welcome to Wales sign. He does

it because as a family this is what we do; my husband because he was born and raised in Newport, and me because whenever I cross the bridge, I am overwhelmed by a deep affection for this land which has been home for over two decades. Hiraeth. The place where I met my husband and birthed a son. A place of hills and coastal lines steeped in meditative beauty. A place where farming communities and post-industrial wastelands face complex new ecological challenges. Wales is as ambiguous as I am. Nation-sanctuary and Brexit-bastion. Made by generations of migrants in the docks and the mines, yet a place that only recognises Welshness as a narrow stereotype. A place in between cultures, looking for a new identity.

On paper, Wales is often described as a place with a strong history of innovation and ingenuity, built on a wealth of multicultural communities. A country small enough to act as a test bed to experiment with different ways of being in the world. More inclusive. More sustainable. More equal. All commitments reflected in legislation brought in by the devolved government these past twenty-five years. Admirable aspirations which clash with the reality of low school attainment and a dire lack of investment all around; with the uncertain direction towards a modern identity that reflects Wales's people – all of its people – beyond the leeks and the rugby games, the chapels and the choirs. A conversation started many times over, and which only serves to showcase a cacophony of contradicting views that appear deaf to one another's view point, warning that Wales could easily fragment along strong polarising lines. I sometimes worry that the latent antagonism against England is a sign of a country that continues to live in the past, justifying a brand of nationalism that would be called racism in any other context, validating exclusionary behaviours that only serve to embed an image of Wales as static, one that bears no resemblance to its stated aspirations.

As a mother, I hope the new Curriculum succeeds in filling the gaps, and that Wales comes to embody a Nation-Sanctuary that makes considerate decisions about its future. A few months back, my son asked if Wales had seemed confusing when I first arrived in the UK. Now that he is older, I can see that he has questions. I look at him and his friends and I notice that he prefers to gravitate towards children with a multicultural background. I do wonder whether this is the result of those well-meaning comments which signal an invisible difference that goes beyond simplistic equal opportunity forms and debates about race, towards broader questions about identity between cultures.

Looking back at my own story, the past twenty-three years have been an exercise in cultural enrichment and constant reframing, so that the identity I embody for my son is a mosaic of the cultures I have traversed and experiences I have faced, whilst Wales is the place that we call home. It is this tension between local and global perspectives which, for me, defines the future in which my son will grow into an adult. A world faced with global ecological challenges that could benefit from hearing stories of adaptation from the 65 million migrants moving between cultures today.

THE POWERS THAT BE: WOMEN IN DEVOLUTION

By Nansi Eccott and Jessica Laimann

Under the devolution settlement, the Senedd and the Welsh Government are responsible for many areas of policymaking in Wales and have implemented hundreds of laws over the past quarter century. As women in Wales are still facing inequality, we will discuss what has been done and what more needs to be done to achieve a Wales free from gender discrimination. Although some positive steps have been made, inequality is still rooted in all many aspects of daily life in post-devolution Wales. This article will look at examples in political representation, heath, childcare, social care, which are some of the key areas devolved to Wales.

Political representation

A key step in fostering equality is to ensure that the voices of women and other underrepresented groups are heard and represented within Wales's legislative bodies. At present, this is not the case and progress over the 25 years of devolution has been mixed.

At inception, the National Assembly for Wales was a leader on women's representation. During the first elections in 1999, women secured 40% of seats. This was closely followed by Scotland, where women gained 37% of seats in the same year, over twice as high as figures for the UK (18% in 1997 general election) and three times as much as Northern Ireland (13% in 1998).[1]

In 2003, Wales became the first, and to date only, UK nation to achieve gender parity in its parliament. The Scottish Parliament was further behind this time at 40%, with the UK and Northern Ireland still failing to hit a meagre 20%. But unfortunately, things have taken a turn for the worse since then.[2] At present, 43% of Senedd Members are women. Although this is an increase of one member from 2016, this figure is not representative of Wales as a whole and makes us rank behind Scotland for the first time since devolution.

In addition to the lack of female members, there is very low representation of people with protected characteristics in the Senedd.[3] At present, there are only three openly LGBTQ+ MSs and we are yet to see any representation from openly trans or non-binary people at Senedd level. The 2021 Senedd election saw the election of the first woman from a racialised background since devolution, Natasha Ashgar MS, who is currently one of only three MSs from an ethnic minority background in the Senedd. Research shows that 43% of Wales's Black, Asian and minority ethnic populations feel that there are not enough positive role models in public and political

---

[1] House of Commons Library (2023), *Women in Politics and Public Life*. https://commonslibrary.parliament.uk/research-briefings/sn01250/

[2] Ibid.

[3] Senedd Research (2021), *Election 2021: How diverse is the Sixth Senedd?* https://research.senedd.wales/research-articles/election-2021-how-diverse-is-the-sixth-senedd/

life and that candidates from these backgrounds face a range of obstacles in running for elected office.[4]

These figures suggest that representation of marginalised groups in the Senedd remains fragile with no safeguards to ensure people from different communities will continue to have a voice. This problem is compounded by a lack of data. Wales has been waiting for more than a decade for the UK Government to commence a section of the Equality Act that would make the collection of anonymised candidate diversity data mandatory.

Fortunately, the ongoing Senedd reform process has provided important opportunities for change. The proposed expansion of the Senedd from 60 to 96 seats for the 2026 election present a once-in-a-lifetime opportunity to bring in voices that are currently underrepresented. In the run-up to it, WEN Wales launched the Diverse 5050 Campaign, calling for legally binding diversity and gender quotas as part of the electoral reform process.

Gender quotas are currently used by over 100 countries worldwide, and research shows that they are the single most effective tool in fast-tracking equal representation.[5] Quotas primarily target one specific barrier to elected office, which is that women and other underrepresented groups can struggle to get shortlisted by political parties. The figures from the 2021 Senedd election suggest that this has a powerful bottleneck effect

---

[4] Race Alliance Wales (2021), *Do the Right Thing: achieving equity in racialised representation in public and political life in Wales,* https://racealliance.wales/wp-content/uploads/2021/01/RAW-Research-paper-160121-2.pdf

[5] Drude Dahlerup et al. (2013), *Atlas of Electoral Gender Quotas, International Institute for Democracy and Electoral Assistance*, IPU and Stockholm University.

on women's representation in Wales. Only 31% of the 470 candidates were women, yet – once selected – they managed to secure 43% of Senedd seats.[6]

The evidence clearly shows that the Welsh Government's commitment to introduce legislative gender quotas for the 2026 elections is a huge step in the right direction. Still, quotas are no silver bullet and are most effective when paired with other measures such as mentoring, job-sharing, support for candidates with caring responsibilities and effective mechanisms to tackle harassment and abuse. While work on some of these measures is underway, whether it will be enough to achieve meaningful change for the 2026 election remains to be seen.

Even when it comes to legislative gender quotas, we are not out of the woods yet. While electoral gender quotas in the Senedd are arguably a question of how Wales wants to run its own elections (a devolved power), the fact that such quotas also touch on equality (a reserved power) has led to concerns over legislative competency. An asymmetry in the UK Equality Act between sex and other protected characteristics means that quotas for groups other than women are currently out of the question. This certainly complicates the fight for quotas, despite sound international evidence, as well as wide support for their introduction among the Senedd, the Welsh Government, and the Welsh public.

---

[6] Senedd Research (2021), *Election 2021: How diverse is the Sixth Senedd?* https://research.senedd.wales/research-articles/election-2021-how-diverse-is-the-sixth-senedd/

Healthcare

Healthcare is another devolved policy area where women in Wales continue to face inequality and discrimination. Women's health conditions are frequently misdiagnosed or dismissed.

Endometriosis affects about one in ten women, yet it takes almost ten years on average to receive a diagnosis in Wales – the longest time in the UK.[7] The recruitment of specialist endometriosis nurses in each health board is an important step forward, but more needs to be done to reduce diagnostic times and to support the many women living with this condition. Due to a lack of professional training and public education, access to appropriate menopause services is equally problematic and often remains a postcode lottery.

Staffing issues in maternity care and a decline in the number of experienced midwives remains another key challenge and one that could potentially compound the risks for mothers from ethnic minority backgrounds.[8] Across the UK, Black women are four times more likely than white women to die during pregnancy or childbirth.[9] The findings also suggest that ethnic minority women experience denial of pain relief due to racial stereotypes,

[7] Endometriosis UK (2024), *"Dismissed, ignored and belittled." The long road to endometriosis diagnosis in the UK.* https://www.endometriosis-uk.org/sites/default/files/2024-03/Endometriosis%20UK%20diagnosis%20survey%202023%20report%20March.pdf

[8] Royal College of Midwives (2023), *State of Maternity Services in Wales,* https://www.rcm.org.uk/media/6898/0246_wales_som_digital.pdf

[9] Birthrights (2021), *New MBRRACE report shows Black women still four times more likely to die in pregnancy and childbirth,* https://www.birthrights.org.uk/2021/11/11/new-mbrrace-report-shows-black-women-still-four-times-more-likely-to-die-in-pregnancy-and-childbirth/

and often feel unsafe and distressed due to pervasive microaggressions.

Case study: Experience of a Black woman giving birth in a Welsh hospital

The birth of my baby was one of the most traumatic experiences I ever had. I was in labour for four days with a baby that was a week overdue. I was in excruciating pain, fighting for my life and that of my baby as I was ignored by health physicians who refused to listen to me each time I told them the pain was unbearable. They kept sending me home. I had two membrane swipes at home which worsened the pain and yet going to the hospital, I was still sent home as I was not dilated enough. I was going out of my mind as the pain worsened and got to the point that I had high fever and was rushed back to the hospital by my husband who was beside himself begging them to help me.

In my pain, struggling to breathe, a nurse asked me to put on a face mask as she did not want to contract Covid even though she was aware that I had tested negative before even being allowed access to the hospital.

There was no blood on standby during the delivery even though my record showed I needed blood on

---

standby in case of an emergency as I was rhesus negative. My husband was almost denied access to me during delivery – the nurse asked him to go outside to do his Covid test whilst a white male was allowed to do his test there and then and have immediate access to his wife.

My husband had to insist on his right before he was allowed. With little or no support, I pushed my baby out and still had no health physician available to stitch me up. It was a healthcare assistant who had to do the job of a physician for me. This experience is something I want no other woman to experience. I deserved better; my baby deserved better.

With health being a devolved policy area, women in Wales are largely relying on the Welsh Government to ensure these issues are being addressed. But while the government has introduced some pioneering work like the Period Proud Action Plan, overall progress has not been as fast as in other UK nations. A 2019 report by the Royal College of Obstetricians and Gynaecologists recommended the creation of women's health plans across the UK.[10] Such work was completed in Scotland

---

[10] Royal College of Obstetricians & Gynaecologists (2019), *Better for women: improving the health and wellbeing of girls and women*, https://www.rcog. org.uk/about-us/campaigning-and-opinions/better-for-women/.

in 2021, and in England in 2022.[11] The Welsh Government committed to follow suit in May 2022, announcing a ten-year plan on women's health. The plan – yet to be finalised – is sorely needed to provide a programme of health services for all stages of life that focuses on the specific needs of women.[12]

Childcare

Unequal caring responsibilities, paired with a lack of affordable childcare, continue to be a driver of stubborn labour market inequalities in Wales. Women make up 86% of single parents in Wales.[13] Even in two-parent households, they continue to carry the bulk of childcare responsibilities, with 63% of mothers saying they are solely or mainly responsible, compared to just 17% of fathers.[14] This means women are much more exposed to pressures within the Welsh childcare system. The current Childcare Offer in Wales, which provides 30 hours a week of early education and childcare for parents of three- and four-year-olds, is a crucial pillar of support. But it only becomes available once key decisions about women's working lives have already been made.

---

[11] Scottish Government (2021), *Women's Health Plan,* https://www.gov.scot/news/womens-health-plan/ and Department of Health and Social Care (2022), *Women's Health Strategy for England,* https://www.gov.uk/government/publications/womens-health-strategy-for-england/womens-health-strategy-for-england.

[12] Welsh Government (2022), *The quality statement for women and girls' health* https://gov.wales/quality-statement-women-and-girls-health-html.

[13] WEN Wales (2022), *Feminist Scorecard 2022,* https://wenwales.org.uk/campaign/feminist-scorecard/.

[14] Ibid.

A lack of affordable childcare causes serious obstacles to women's efforts to seek and progress in employment, often resulting in a stunt in career development and lifetime financial inequalities. Between October 2022 and September 2023, 38% of women worked part time, compared to 13% of men, and 26% of women were economically inactive compared to 20% of men.[15] Among those who were economically inactive, more than a quarter (26%) of women, but only 7% of men, cited looking after the family or home as the main reason.[16]

Funded childcare provisions for three- and four-year-olds in the range of 30 hours per week are provided in England, Scotland and Wales. In Wales and England, the full 30 hours are only available to working parents, with a recent expansion in Wales to those in education and training. In Northern Ireland, three- and four-year-olds are entitled to only 12.5 hours per week of free pre-school education.

Entitlements for younger children are more varied. England provides 15 hours of free childcare to two-year-olds if the child is care-experienced, has additional learning needs or if the parents are in receipt of qualifying benefits. From April 2024, the same provision will be available to working parents. In Scotland, eligible two-year-olds can get 30 hours of free childcare if the children are care-experienced, or parents are in receipt of qualifying benefits.

---

[15] Office for National Statistics (2023), *Annual Population Survey*, Oct 2022 - Sep 2023, retrieved via NOMIS on 4 March 2024, https://www.nomisweb.co.uk/articles/1336.aspx.

[16] Ibid.

In Wales, free childcare for two-year-olds is provided under the Flying Start scheme, which was originally only available in areas classed as most disadvantaged and is currently being rolled out to all two-year-olds in Wales. The scheme, which provides 12.5 hours of childcare, delivered as 2.5 hours per day over five days, has been criticised as a 'postcode lottery' and as being too restricted to support parental employment. With both England and Scotland having committed to a more generous expansion over the coming years, Wales is under pressure to follow suit.

Being entitled to government-funded childcare does not guarantee that parents will be able to access a place. In comparison with England and Scotland, childcare sufficiency in Wales is the lowest across a range of demographics and entitlements.[17] For the funded entitlements for three- and four-year-olds, the percentage of local authorities who reported sufficient provision across their authority in 2023 was 94% in Scotland, 66% in England and only 37% in Wales.[18] Over the same period, no local authority in Wales was able to report sufficient childcare across all areas for either disabled children, parents working atypical hours or families in rural areas.

Social care and unpaid care

The gendered dynamics and challenges around care work do not stop with children. In the social care sector,

---

[17] Coram Family and Chilcare (2023), *Childcare Survey 2023*, https://www.familyandchildcaretrust.org/childcare-survey-2023-report-landing-page.

[18] Ibid.

women make up 82% of the workforce, with racialised women being overrepresented in the lowest paying and most insecure roles.[19] Their work is vital to the health and well-being of the Welsh population, which has been recognised in commendable initiatives, such as the introduction of the real living wage for social care workers in Wales. Yet the sector remains in crisis. Due to staffing challenges, people's support needs across the country often cannot be met.

This has disastrous knock-on effects on health services, as well as on unpaid carers, who provide around 96% of care work in Wales. Nearly 60% of unpaid carers in Wales are women.[20] Over a quarter of unpaid carers describe their mental health as bad or very bad and many are struggling to make ends meet.[21] Although the Government has committed to an investment of £4.5 million to support unpaid carers during the cost-of-living crisis, this figure pales in comparison to the £33 million that unpaid carers are estimated to save the Welsh economy on a daily basis.[22]

---

[19] Social Care Wales (2022), Social care workforce report
https://socialcare.wales/cms-assets/documents/Social-care-workforce-report-2022.pdf.

[20] Huang, F. et al. (2021). *Unpaid carers in Wales: The determinants of mental wellbeing*. Cardiff: Public Health Wales NHS Trust,
https://phw.nhs.wales/publications/publications1/unpaid-carers-in-wales-the-determinants-of-mental-wellbeing/.

[21] Carers Wales (2023), State of Caring 2023,
https://www.carersuk.org/media/wrnfh0mg/sociw23-health-design-final-eng-compressed.pdf.

[22] Welsh Government (2022), *New fund launched to support unpaid carers in Wales during the cost of living crisis*, https://media.service.gov.wales/news/grants-of-up-to-gbp-300-to-be-available-to-unpaid-carers-in-wales-to-support-them-during-the-cost-of-living-crisis.

We are still a long way away from ensuring unpaid care work truly becomes a choice and that paid care work is valued in accordance with its importance. Affordable, high-quality social care and childcare is not just a key pillar of gender equality. It is the invisible infrastructure that holds up our economy and society and should therefore be at the heart of the Welsh Government's response to the cost-of-living crisis and the transition to a net zero economy.[23]

Conclusion

While the Welsh Government has taken many positive steps to tackle gender inequality in devolved areas, a lot more remains to be done. Wales has long been a leader amongst the four nations in equal representation, but progress will continue to be undone if we do not take urgent steps now. Gendered health inequalities is an area where Wales appears to be lagging behind as women continue to await the introduction of a dedicated women's health plan for Wales. Across the childcare and social care sector, positive work has been done but the experience in other devolved nations shows that more is possible.

While the areas discussed above are devolved, meaning that powers over legislative and policy change lie largely with the Welsh Government, its efforts to promote gender equality often face serious restrictions. There are, for once, Wales's very limited fiscal powers, which set

---

[23]WEN Wales (2023), *Make Care Fair Briefing*, https://wenwales.org.uk/wp-content/uploads/2023/09/Make-Care-Fair.WenWales.3.pdf.

boundaries to possible investments into areas where they are sorely needed, such as childcare and social care.

In addition, equality as policy area is currently not devolved – as are other areas that dramatically shape women's everyday lives, such as welfare, justice, and immigration. Lack of devolved powers means that progressive initiatives cannot always easily be delivered in a way that would maximise their impact. For instance, the Violence against Women, Domestic Abuse and Sexual Violence (VAWDASV) (Wales) Act 2015 aims to tackle the root causes of gender-based violence and protect and support those affected through a whole-system approach. This would require the effective collaboration of devolved and non-devolved bodies, including police and courts, in line with the stated objectives, which is not always a given under the current settlement.

Over the past years, the Welsh Government has made commitments that aspire for Wales to be a nation that is feminist, anti-racist, the most LGBTQ+ friendly nation in Europe, a nation of sanctuary, the safest place in Europe to be a woman, and a nation that is committed to the social model of disability. Every single one of these ambitions is laudable, and concrete steps towards advancing them at a devolved level are being progressed through various action plans and taskforces. But it is difficult to see how these ambitions can be truly realised without the power to pass legislation that allows Wales to do things differently, or to go above and beyond, what the current UK legislative permits in key reserved areas.

There is reason to believe that the devolution of further

fiscal and legislative powers could help advance the fight for gender equality in Wales. All the while, despite ambitious commitments and some pioneering activity, progress in areas that are already devolved has not always met expectations. Work needs to continue to ensure devolved powers are put to best use to advance gender equality, and that those in charge of deploying and scrutinising them truly represent women in their full diversity in Welsh society.

About WEN Wales

At the Women's Equality Network (WEN) Wales, our vision is a Wales free from gender discrimination where everyone has equal authority and opportunity to shape society and their own lives. We connect, campaign and champion to bring women's voices together, call out gender inequality and celebrate inspirational women.

VANISHING ACTS

By Jasmine Donahaye

When I started learning Welsh in 1998, I had been living in California for nine years. The Celtic Studies degree at UC Berkeley was reconnecting me to Britain, where I'd grown up – but it seemed a Britain about to be transformed by the passage of the Government of Wales Act earlier that year.

In many subjects at Berkeley the research and teaching leads the world, but our Welsh texts were rather out of date. For the module in Medieval Welsh, we used a red clothbound hardback edition of *Pwyll* published in Dublin in 1986; for Modern Welsh we used a 1990 edition of *Cymraeg i Ddysgwyr: Welsh for Learners*, originally published in 1978. The 1990 edition differed little from its predecessor, because, as the introductory note explained, 'no major changes were thought necessary in a publication which has been in demand for the last ten years'.[1]

Through the first hot weeks of the autumn semester, with all the windows open to the riotous noise of the UC Berkeley campus, I sat for hours struggling to translate sentences such as 'she likes shopping' and 'she'll buy lamb for the weekend,' and laughing at the accompanying line drawings, which featured stories about a straight

---

[1] *Cymraeg i Ddysgwyr: Welsh for Learners* (Foxgate Ltd, 1990).

179

white nuclear family, and a straight white couple. The women in the images iron; the men drive ('Ble ydyn ni'n mynd nawr, Gwilym?' asks Megan). There is an exception, though, when Megan drives: she reverses into a bin and scratches the car. 'How are you going to tell Dad?' says their daughter.

Of course, this book offered an absurdly inaccurate picture, I thought. At a distance of some 5000 miles, I had formed an idealistic view that Welsh culture was egalitarian, progressive and enlightened – and with devolution it was about to realise its full potential.

Nothing I knew, other than that out-of-date textbook, really challenged my belief. I had been spared English stereotypes of Wales because though I'd grown up in Sussex I'd lived most of my adulthood abroad. Before I'd left England, Wales was present in my imagination as a place, not a culture. I'd visited twice in the early 70s, when my parents crammed my siblings and me into the backseat of our red Hillman Husky, and my father drove us from Sussex to Ceredigion for our summer holidays. I'd also been twice as an adult to a farm in Pembrokeshire. The early family visits were shaped by birdwatching, the later ones by landscape.

After I moved to Wales in early 2002, my belief that the country was in a state of exciting development coloured everything I encountered. After all, here was the first parliament in the world that was 50% women (albeit briefly). This was a culturally expansive, outward-looking, socially responsible place; it was a time of potential, of opportunities opening up for everyone.

My view of the country during those apparently confident, optimistic years of early devolution could only have been possible, perhaps, because my sense of Wales developed primarily in an academic, literary and cultural milieu, and at one remove. I could romanticise y cefn gwlad, where I was living, as an idealised repository of open and tolerant Welsh-language culture because I wasn't part of it. I did not have to acknowledge that it was also a tangle of corruption, ugly family rivalries, political entrenchment, hostility to outsiders and, above all, narrowly prescribed roles for women. As for working-class industrial Wales – or, more accurately post-industrial south Wales – I was at an even greater remove: it came to me through Welsh literature in English from the 1920s and 30s, just as my sense of rural Wales came to me through the filter of north Wales fiction in translation.

Nevertheless, my rosy picture of y cefn gwlad didn't survive for very long. Perhaps that Welsh learner's textbook really hadn't needed major revisions, I realised, because it turned out that those 1978 line drawings were quite an accurate portrait after all – at least in terms of gender. Despite the early promise of equal representation in government, it became apparent that a higher profile for women was only supported and tolerated so long as it didn't upset the old order.

So much had seemed possible, at first. During the early years of devolved government, funding for literature and publishing grew generously, and new cultural policy was full of promise. It was a period of confident investigation of Wales's past, and there was an explosion of innovative thought and expression in the field of literature and publishing in which I was engaged. The growth of academic research in Welsh writing in English mirrored the transfer from the Arts Council to the Welsh Books Council (as it was then) of the English-language literature grant, which was followed by the allocation of additional funding, including support for the new classics publications series, the Library of Wales. In academic fields, and in popular writing, researchers were uncovering a depth of previously overlooked cultural material, including the recovery of invisible women. Yet even while the contribution of women had become better understood and recognised, a more lasting acknowledgement remained conditional, and separate.

I imagine that the rediscovery of invisible women is possible or even probable in most fields of research, because whatever their contribution, women disappear from view, or are actively vanished. There does not seem any more concise way than this transitive use of the verb 'to vanish' to capture this process that renders a woman invisible. Although the transitive form feels clunky, its very clunkiness highlights how this vanishing is a deliberate act rather than a passive effect. Perhaps the echo of the brand-name *Vanish* is also helpful, in that it suggests both stain removal and the domestic world to which a woman is restricted when she's excluded from the record.[2]

---

[2] To make this a transitive form might seem to dangerously echo linguistically with the transitive form of 'to disappear', given the state-sponsored violence enacted against 'The Disappeared'. But while to vanish women is in itself not a violent act against the person, it contributes to an environment in which violence against women is enabled.

However, it is not sufficient to rediscover the work of women who have been vanished in this way. Despite such discoveries, the values that determine who represents the past for the present continue to erase.

I had not expected to discover a forgotten woman writer during my doctoral research, which focused on Welsh Jewish writing, but there she was in plain sight when I looked: noted in her time, and then forgotten. When a woman also does not belong to a country's ethnic majority, that disappearance is even more inevitable.

Lily Tobias had been celebrated between the two world wars. She was published by major English presses in the 1930s, and was a prominent figure, first in the Cardiff cultural milieu and then in leftwing London literary circles. In her four novels (*Eunice Fleet*, *My Mother's House*, *Tube* and *The Samaritan*) she combined the style of the popular modern romance, typical of a post-war generation of women writers, with the political struggle that typified the proletarian fiction of her contemporary, Lewis Jones. Like Jones, she struggled to find a literary voice that could convey the pathos of human experience and the pungency of political statement. Written against the imperative of modernist literary innovation in that interwar period, and unique in its political focus, particularly in its comparisons of Welsh and Jewish national aspirations, her fiction fused the modern romance with the heightened drama of political idealism, exploring the ways that political engagement played out in individual rather than collective struggles. But by the time of her death in 1984, Tobias had been forgotten. Instead of obituaries, she was accorded one small paragraph in the *Jewish Chronicle*, sent in by her nephew Dannie Abse, though she had been a contributor to the newspaper well beyond the middle of the twentieth century.

That disappearance from view was typical of the fate of so many women writers of the interwar period who did not fit into the narrow categories by which they were permitted to achieve lasting recognition. Tobias's work was neither modernist nor radical in style, and after she moved to British Mandate Palestine in the 1930s her books went out of print and were forgotten. That move to Palestine at precisely the moment of her literary arrival contributed to her erasure as a writer in the UK, but even without it she would almost certainly have disappeared from view. As Angela Ingram and Daphne Patai so succinctly put it about a whole generation of radical women writers in the 1930s whose political focus rendered them quickly unfashionable: their concern 'was not to find new ways to express new forms of consciousness but rather to expose the resilience of old forms of consciousness that prevailed then and that still prevail today'.[3] That observation was made by them in 1993, but it still seems true some thirty years on.

In 2005 Lewis Jones's *Cwmardy* and *We Live* were included in the first five books of the Library of Wales series, the ambitious nation-building publishing endeavour that sought to represent Wales to itself and to

---

[3] Angela Ingram and Daphne Patai (eds), *Rediscovering Forgotten Radicals: British Women Writers 1889-1939* (Chapel Hill: University of North Carolina Press, 1993), p. 9.

the world. Lily Tobias, Jones's contemporary, remains excluded, like so many other women writers. The inequality of representation in the first tranche of the series – one text by a woman and eight by men – was the subject of heated public and private debate at the time. This disparity was purportedly because those women who would have been acceptable (Menna Gallie, for example) had already been republished in Honno's Welsh Women's Classics series. However, the next few years did little to right the balance.[4]

When I suggested Tobias for inclusion, she was rejected on aesthetic grounds – aesthetic grounds which, it would appear, did not apply to Lewis Jones's novels, peopled as they are by didactic political mouthpieces. Somehow Jones's work met some standard that Tobias's did not reach. Evidently a different set of aesthetic criteria were being used to judge her work.

Perhaps the political and ethnic minority preoccupations of Tobias's works, which informed such aesthetic judgements, did not fit the narrative of the national past that was being shaped for the present in those early years of devolution, but she was only one of many woman writers considered not quite up to par for Library of Wales inclusion. Like these other awkward women, Tobias would still be invisible if it had not been for the intervention of Honno, who republished two of her novels, and commissioned a biography.

Her own nephew, Dannie Abse, whose novel *Ash on a*

---

[4] I served as Project Editor of the Library of Wales from its inception to 2007, and was responsible for the production side.

Young Man's Sleeve was the ninth Library of Wales volume, had once described Tobias's work to me dismissively as 'middlebrow'. Following Honno's publication of her 1931 novel *Eunice Fleet*, about conscientious objectors, he acknowledged that he'd been unfair in this dismissal. The tapestry of Welsh heritage is the more richly patterned for that recognition by Honno, and our understanding of it is deepened.

The omission of women from the Library of Wales series outraged me at the time, and outraged many others whose research in the field of Welsh writing in English was contributing to a more representative version of the Welsh past. The Library of Wales series offered such a straightforward opportunity to right the balance in the present, and it was bypassed.

This particular example is a useful indication in the present of how women have been vanished in the past. It is not enough simply to rediscover and acknowledge in passing the overlooked historical contributions of women as a means of correcting the record. Without lasting public forms of recognition in the present – with equal rather than separate representation – those women disappear from view again, and this undermines the possibility of equal representation in the future.

Looking back, it's clear how in that post-devolution moment of cultural expansion, old familiar patterns were being reinforced in new ways. The standards that women had to meet in order to merit recognition and inclusion were still much more demanding and narrowly defined than those for men, and women's contributions continued to be segregated, and thus vulnerable to erasure. Men were still driving; women were still relegated to the passenger seat.

In 2015, when Honno republished Tobias's powerful second novel in conjunction with the biography they had commissioned me to write about her, I was taken aback when readers repeatedly asked how she could have fallen from view. It seemed to strike people as something unusual, when in fact such vanishing acts have been so typical for women in general, and women writers in particular.[5]

Nearly a century on from her disappearance, evidence of continued inequality is visible everywhere if you choose to look. Still, it's hard to see an invisibility until you look for it: that invisibility has to move from being an 'unknown unknown' to a 'known unknown', to adapt Donald Rumsfeld's awkward risk-assessment formulation.

When I turned to public statues that summer as a physical illustration of such vanishing acts, I wondered what it was that women had to do in order to merit the lasting recognition that men enjoy in public space, both metaphorically and physically. As I found out, here it wasn't just a case of inequality: it was a case of total invisibility. There were any number of men making grand and heroic gestures, fixed for perpetuity on plinths in town squares and civic buildings throughout Wales, but

---

[5] One need only take a cursory look at the historical VIDA Count statistics, beginning in 2009, to see how these patterns have continued to play out, with disproportionate numbers of male editors, male reviewers, and male writers reviewed across the print media. See https://www.vidaweb.org/the-count/previous-counts/.

when I tried to visualise a comparable statue of a woman, I could not recall a single one. Nor could anyone else, after I enquired on social media – because there were none. Four years earlier, public historian Sara Huws had made the same observation about public sculpture in Cardiff.[6]

With the exception of Queen Victoria (who was not memorialised for what she did, but for what she was), statues of women in Wales were restricted to symbolic or mythical roles in churches, war memorials and courts: there were madonnas, and some embodiments of Truth or Justice or Peace, as well as one Boudicea, and an anonymous anti-war group representing Greenham Common – but there was not a single publicly sited statue of a named individual woman that commemorated her for what she had done. Women still had to serve as symbols or inherit a crown to merit public representation: there were no real women to physically look up to or navigate by, no women to name and acknowledge.

When I made this observation, and suggested that it was time to rectify the omission, it became a popular news item.[7] This should have been a warning sign, because despite reporting by the BBC, and many media opportunities to discuss the absence of women statues, the problem and its solution never moved into the development of policy that would seek to address the causes and consequences of that historical vanishing act. Nor, as far as I know, was there any public policy, then or since, to proactively prevent its recurrence in the future.

---

[6] See https://sarahuws.wordpress.com/2011/03/28/a-modest-proposal/.

[7] See for example https://www.bbc.co.uk/news/uk-wales-33497685.

Instead, the question of women statues got taken up as a popular public campaign – what the writer Mike Parker went on to characterise caustically as a beauty contest.[8]

This intervention of the Hidden Heroines campaign, organised by the group Monumental Welsh Women, supported by the BBC, and launched in 2016 at the National Eisteddfod, managed to change the landscape a little.[9] But it also illustrated how the memorialisation of women in this way was only possible when it didn't really challenge the status quo, but simply filled a historic gap. Regrettably, this is much what Honno's Welsh Women's Classics series does too. It's a safe solution, because it lets everyone else off the hook. This way we can pretend that either the gap was never there in the first place, or we can pretend that the problem which caused the gap has been addressed.

The men who persist on pedestals were never held to the standard that the women selected in the Hidden Heroines campaign have been held, either in what they achieved, or in who admired them. They were deemed important by virtue of the esteem in which they were held by their equally powerful peers. It's true that by late 2023, thanks to the Monumental Welsh Women campaign, and limited financial support from the government, the country had

---

[8] Mike Parker, 'Ironic that to get one single statue of an actual woman in Cardiff, we have to conduct a glorified beauty contest to decide who it's going to be.' Twitter, 8 January 2019. See also Jasmine Donahaye, 'We shouldn't let the only statue of a woman in Wales become a monument to continued inequality', https://nation.cymru/opinion/betty-campbell-statue-jasmine-donahaye/ 5 February 2019, and Jasmine Donahaye, 'Statue No. 1', BBC Radio 4, 9 October 2019. https://www.bbc.co.uk/programmes/m00088jm.

[9] For information on the statues, see https://monumentalwelshwomen.com/the-statues.

three publicly sited statues of real women to look up to, with two more to come, but this has only occurred after the very value of commemorative statues has been questioned and challenged.

Here again, Ingram and Patai's observations from 1993 about the political women writers of the 1930s are as pertinent now as they were thirty years ago. 'Is it a coincidence,' they ask in the introduction to *Rediscovering Forgotten Radicals*, 'that only recently, as women and other people labeled "minorities" have approached the literary banquet table, the status of *all* diners at the table has been thrown into doubt?'[10]

Statues are being pulled down or vandalised or moved. We understand better that many of the individuals memorialised in this way represent worldviews and behaviour that we can no longer admire. We also recognise that such statues represent an exercise of power that is now objectionable. It is only when this very legitimacy of putting anyone on a pedestal is in question that a statue of a real woman in Wales has been made possible. And it not only coincides with the value of statues being in doubt: it also occurs after the very categories of gender and biological sex have become contested.

Supported only when the potential impact of the change has been undermined, the statues of Betty Campbell, Elaine Morgan and Cranogwen, and of those still to come, will stand as monuments to continued inequality as much as they stand as monuments to these women's achievements. Having fought for the right to an

---

[10] Ingram and Patai, p. 9.

equal seat at the table, we have been admitted to the banquet only to find that the meal has already been eaten and the other guests have left.

I think of that textbook, *Cymraeg i Ddysgwyr*, through which I first encountered Welsh culture, and wonder what kinds of revisions it would need to undergo in order to reflect the Wales of the present. Of course it would require major amendments to accommodate the profound linguistic and demographic changes that have taken place in the last three decades, and to more accurately depict the diverse ethnic makeup of the country, both past and present. But there are so many ways in which those line drawings of the man in the driving seat and the woman as a passenger are still more true than many of us would care to admit – even if we are pointing out that he's missed the turning and is heading into a dead end.

OPENING DOORS AND BREAKING DOWN BARRIERS: WOMEN, EDUCATION, AND DEVOLUTION

By Dr Michelle Deininger

I don't think it's much of a stretch to say that education saved me. There have been multiple points in my life where engagement with education outside of school, from part-time college provision to lifelong learning within a university setting, gave me the chance to find my own voice – and to have hope. When you come from a working-class background, where generations have been steeped in poverty, and hardly anyone stays on for sixth form, let alone goes to university, it's hard to see what you might become.

A PhD and a university lecturing job certainly didn't feature in my dreams for the future. My old estate of Blackbird Leys, in Oxford, made the news in 2016 when a Freedom of Information Act request revealed that no students from the most deprived areas of Oxford (Blackbird Leys and Northfield Brook) had been awarded a place at Oxford in over a decade. Articles often focus on this false dichotomy of who has made it to the dreaming spires when it should be about accessing higher education at all. I will say, when those spires are on your doorstep and you can't come in, it's a kick in the teeth that you feel every time you cross Magdalen Bridge on the Number 5 bus on the way into town. (And you'll never fully understand why the bridge is spelt one way and pronounced more like 'Maudlen'.) What caught my attention more from that article was the point that only 7.5% of young people were recorded as entering higher education before the age of nineteen between 2005-2011. My time there was a little earlier, but I would have been part of that small minority – and I lasted at my university for exactly two months before dropping out. I wouldn't restart my journey for some time.

That experience shaped so much of my twenties – that deeply-held belief that education was not for me and that I did not belong. Years later, when I worked in a role that explored how to retain students in higher education, I discovered that dropping out was pretty much locked into my future outcomes – that students from areas like mine, often eligible for free school meals, were at the highest risk of leaving education early. And again, when I returned to higher education in 2005, with two small children in tow and a direct entrant to year two of my degree, I was yet again within an 'at risk' group. Some of this was tied up in that feeling of not belonging, of not being a 'traditional' entrant to higher education. However, much of the problem lies with universities that have poor induction processes for entrants that arrive in any other year apart from the first. And many don't have well-funded provision for the induction of mature students – something I've helped fight for and provide in my current role as a university lecturer. My own induction involved a senior tutor passing me a timetable and leaving me to it. I ended up crying on an administrative assistant in the student records office as I had no idea how to fill in the forms required to register on my chosen modules. I went back and thanked her years later, when I started teaching at the university myself – without that kindness, I might have walked out the door and never come back. How many do just this, I often wonder to myself. How many barriers should working-class students have to break down before they can finally come in?

Beyond belonging, some of the reasons for being 'at risk' were deeply entwined with money. The first time I went to university, I remember continually asking at the university's finance counter about my grant cheque – the only income I had for the year, without taking out a student loan. Due to an administrative error, the cheque never arrived and I eventually got the portion of the grant I was entitled to *after* I dropped out. I can't go back far enough in my digital student finance account to see how much this was, but I think it was a couple of hundred pounds. I don't know if there were errors with the way my application was handled or if I did something wrong when I applied, but there was nothing like the promised amount for students based in London, which was supposed to be paid at a higher rate. As the first in my family to complete compulsory secondary education, there was no one to ask. I assumed the authorities knew best. This kind of lack of knowledge is a huge barrier and is something I strive to offset in the work I do with adult learners in my role as a lecturer in Lifelong Learning.

Adequate income for studying is key and this is

something that devolution in Wales helps support. When I was looking back over my student finance record, I noticed that in 2004 I had support from Student Finance England for my course, a Foundation Certificate in English Language and Literature from Oxford University's Department for Continuing Education (OUDCE). The first year of my course, I had received a fee waiver due to being on a low income. The second year, this scheme was abolished and support had to be applied for from the local authority. Luckily, OUDCE were very much aware of the impact this could have on low-income students and ensured full information and support was provided so that I could continue my studies. Without that support, I would have been in limbo, unable to afford the tuition fee. Two years previously, I had taken a night class in A level Philosophy that gave me a stepping stone back into learning. It was a tricky couple of years, which included the birth of my second child in the third week of the second year. I'd had some kind of fee waiver for that course, too, again due to low income. While the tuition fees weren't huge, they were a barrier. In effect, my re-entry into education was free to access – this made it possible.

All of my experiences had been within the English system and it was not until I started to teach in the Welsh sector, including in both higher education and further education, that I started to see the difference between the funding model in Wales compared to England. I think it's fair to say that the devolved Welsh system is far more generous, from Education Maintenance Allowance (EMA) for sixth formers (Wales was the first country to increase

EMA rates in 2023) to maintenance grants for part-time undergraduate-level courses, with additional loans if needed. (Master's maintenance grants, on the other hand, are being replaced with loans for 2024/25, in line with England – a disappointing policy shift.) In England, part-time university students can only access a loan for maintenance, so students are building a higher level of debt as soon as their studies begin. In Wales, students who earn £25,000 a year or less can access a £3,000 grant. The impact of this on women, especially those who are balancing caring responsibilities and more likely to be working part-time as a result, is potentially huge. For women earning the minimum wage, currently £10.42 per hour (2023/24 rates, over 23 years of age), having access to the grant would give them the potential to reduce their working hours by approximately five hours a week. This genuinely creates space and time for study. Students who are parents can also apply for Childcare Grants and Parents' Learning Allowance – more grants that do not have to be repaid. While there can be an impact on Universal Credit, for the most part the benefits of this financial package outweigh the negatives. Across the funding package, Wales provides its students with a fairer offering compared to England. For full-time undergraduates, there has been a Student Finance Partial Cancellation Scheme in place for many years. The Welsh Government will cancel up to £1,500 from any full-time maintenance loan balance when students enter repayment. While this may not seem like much, it does help to reduce overall debt and, more importantly, incentivises finishing a course. Wales was also cautious about raising full-time tuition fees for undergraduates to £9,000 per year and has not raised them beyond that level since they first reached that figure – a decision that has caused much difficulty to the Welsh HE sector itself as it has to do more work with less tuition fee income. Whether this will be sustainable in the future remains to be seen. The decision to slash fees for Foundation Years (an extra year added on to a standard degree for students who do not meet the standard entry requirements, often popular with mature students) in England raises so many questions about the longer-term sustainability of 'non-traditional' routes.

Reflecting on my experiences has enabled me to look more broadly on the opportunities available in Wales, especially for adults returning to learning, as I did. One key aspect, I believe, is having the opportunity to undertake learning without much (or any) financial risk. This is where devolution has had a significant impact on adult learners in Wales as there has been the opportunity for shaping policy so that it fits the needs of its citizens. In my role as a lecturer in Lifelong Learning, I see the impact money has on my students all the time. 'I can't afford to study,' a potential student will say to me. And my answer will always be, 'Have you seen the package that Student Finance Wales offers its students?' Part-time adult learners in Wales currently receive a £500 grant whatever level of income they might have, and will often be eligible for grants I've mentioned already, in the region of £3000 (for courses at half the intensity of undergraduate full time courses), if they are within the lower income brackets. This kind of funding means that a parent with kids can come to evening classes, via Cardiff University's Pathway to a Degree programme scheme (which offers a route for mature students into degrees at Cardiff University and beyond) and end up on a degree in nursing a year later. Equally, it opens up the chance for disabled students to study part-time, at their own pace, via the Open University, perhaps taking an English degree and then moving on to teacher training (also available via the OU in Wales). These are just two (real) examples from two institutions, but they demonstrate the breadth of opportunities available to Welsh residents, and the doors that can open when people make the decision to step back into the classroom, whether virtual, physical or via distance learning. I've seen the difference having these opportunities can make, the way that lives change, and the confidence that grows. I see it especially in the women I have supported, who are often battling with negative experiences from school, which has left them feeling 'stupid', or simply not having the chance to find the subject they really enjoy.

What's even more forward thinking in Wales is that if you are already a degree holder, you can apply for funding for a second, part-time undergraduate degree in certain shortage areas, mostly taken from Science, Technology, Engineering and Maths, as well as environmentally focused courses. History has snuck onto the list of eligible courses provided by the Open University, though, as has Philosophical and

Psychological Studies – there is still some space for the humanities, something which is fundamentally vital. As it currently stands, parents with children who are in receipt of Student Finance Wales funding can apply for student finance themselves for a second degree and their income will not be counted. (I only know this as I started studying undergraduate level Environmental Studies with the Open University last year after I began to take a deeper interest in the climate crisis. I've already got three degrees and two standalone postgraduate courses under my belt – I don't think I'll ever stop learning.) These kinds of policy decisions open doors, encourage people back into learning and potentially back into the workforce. They also, and this is key, give women the chance to start or restart their learning journeys, when their time has often been taken up with caring responsibilities, whether that's children or elderly relatives. Getting a £3,000 grant to study, when the mortgage has gone up (thanks partly to the mistakes made by the short-lived Truss government) or the kids need help to pay their student accommodation, makes the idea of studying possible. At the other end of the scale, Student Finance Wales also supports students who are at a very different life stage, offering tuition fee loans for both full-time and part-time study with no upper age limit. Again, this makes studying possible, but for students who return to education much later in life.

It's not just degrees that Welsh funding policies support. The fee waivers that I mentioned earlier are still doing excellent work to encourage students back into education. One of the most transformational changes I have witnessed myself is the expansion of the criteria for fee waivers for up to 20 credits in standalone courses at Cardiff University, within my own Division. Funded by the Higher Education Funding Council for Wales (HEFCW), this scheme has traditionally been accessed by learners with disabilities or those in receipt of certain income-based benefits. Over the last two academic years, the criteria have been widened to include applicants from groups underrepresented in higher education, including Black, Asian or minority ethnic applicants, carers, care leavers, asylum seekers, refugees, and LGBTQ+ applicants. When I have a potential student in front of me who isn't ready to study at the intensity needed to undertake something like the Pathways to a Degree scheme, but wants to study something, I have an option for them. 'How would you like to do some learning *for free*?' I ask. Often those students are women – women who have been excluded from mainstream education, lacking confidence due to poor educational experiences, discouraged by online learning during the pandemic, unable to access daytime courses due to having small children, disengaged from education because of gender presentation or sexual identity, wanting an online course due to a disability, or being pulled in different directions by caring for elderly relatives. These are just a small number of examples. Now I have something I can offer them, with no risk – aside from developing a passion for learning, of course.

The Open University in Wales has also provided

excellent courses with fee waivers attached, including their microcredential in Online Teaching: Creating Courses for Adult Learners, which was offered to Cardiff University staff for free during the latter stages of the pandemic. (Obviously, I took this course – as a lifelong learner myself, I couldn't turn down the opportunity. And, like many people, I didn't have a spare £675 to spend on this and improve my skills without the fee waiver.) This microcredential was again funded by HEFCW, a body that will soon become the Commission for Tertiary Education and Research (CTER), covering both Further and Higher Education. As a Lifelong Learning professional, I cannot overstate how important it is to have genuine access to education without financial strings attached. In a society that fully believes in everyone reaching their full potential, funding opportunities shouldn't stop with supporting the most vulnerable – it should offer something for everyone, including professionals who need and want to upskill. More broadly, the establishment of CTER opens up the chance for genuine synergy between FE and HE, with funding that works across sectors, and the opportunity to break down some of the hierarchical barriers between post-16, community, adult, and university education. I look forward to seeing what this new commission will bring to Welsh education, and the opportunities it will open up.

My own journey through education as an adult, which has been punctuated by varying degrees of poverty, has been supported, facilitated, and ultimately enriched by access to free education. When you come from a working-class background, taking that initial step without a financial risk is key. Cardiff University's *Live Local, Learn Local* programme, which offers level 3 courses (roughly equivalent to A level or BTEC study but in small, bitesize chunks) and is supported by the Reaching Wider initiative, is completely free to access. Similarly, Cardiff Metropolitan University provides free Widening Access courses, including some excellent summer school schemes in subjects like Creative Writing. The Open University has a suite of preparatory Access modules, across a broad range of subject areas – 80% of students are able to access these modules for free. This is a very different model to the Lifelong Learning loan which is receiving much attention in England – loans, of course, have to be repaid. Free education, on the other hand, does not come with a price tag attached.

The establishment of The Well-being of Future Generations (Wales) Act 2015 has provided a way in which to embed a multitude of different aspects of everyday life into the fabric of Welsh legislation, intrinsically linking them with access to education. The fact that we have this legislation at all is due to devolution. The Act emphasises the importance of Wales being prosperous, resilient, healthier, more equal, having cohesive communities, a vibrant culture and thriving Welsh language, and a nation that is globally responsible. All of these elements are improved by access to education. I've focused predominantly in this piece on the experiences of women, mainly because the women I have supported and worked with over my career to date have often had the most difficult journeys to undertake when they've come back into education. And they resonate with my own. I often think back to a piece I read when I was taking my Foundation Certificate at Oxford University – *A Room of One's Own* (1929) by Virgina Woolf. She made the argument that women need £500 a year and a room of their own to be able to write. The argument also stands, with some steep inflation to offset the cost of living crisis, to study and gain an education. The image that has always stuck with me is when Woolf describes trying to access the library at a semi-fictional Oxford or Cambridge, having first attempted to cross the grass in a college quad. Chased by an intimidating member of college staff, she is not allowed on the grass. Neither is she allowed into the college library without a letter of introduction or being accompanied by a (male) fellow of the college. While these kinds of barriers have shifted hugely since the 1920s, and women's rights to education have become fully enshrined in law, there are still closed doors to push open, and material and psychological barriers to overturn and break through. A devolved Wales means that we can make these kinds of choices for ourselves as a nation – to build fairness and equality into the way we fund education. Ensuring there is access to opportunities for Welsh people to study, to learn, and to embrace new ways of thinking should be at the heart of decision making and education policies for all learners, whatever their age. This should be one of the most significant and transformative legacies of devolution – and I hope it will continue to be in the decades to come.

List of resources

Fee waivers at Cardiff University's Lifelong Learning
Division – https://www.cardiff.ac.uk/part-time-
courses-for-adults/courses/funding-and-paying-for-your
-learning

Cardiff University's Pathways to a Degree –
https://www.cardiff.ac.uk/part-time-courses-for-
adults/pathways-to-a-degree

Free widening access courses at Cardiff Metropolitan
University – https://www.cardiffmet.ac.uk/
study/wideningaccess/Pages/default.aspx

Oxford University Department for Continuing
Education (OUDCE –) https://www.conted.ox.ac.uk/

Education Maintenance Allowance (Wales) –
https://www.studentfinancewales.co.uk/further-
education-funding/education-maintenance-allowance/

Student Finance Wales
     Part-time undergraduate funding – https://www.
     studentfinancewales.co.uk/undergraduate-
     finance/part-time/

     Eligibility for part-time funding –
     https://www.studentfinancewales.co.uk/undergradu
     ate-finance/part-time/welsh-student/who-qualifies/

     Full-time undergraduate funding –
     https://www.studentfinancewales.co.uk/undergradu
     ate-finance/full-time/

Eligibility for full-time undergraduate funding – https://www.studentfinancewales.co.uk/undergradu ate-finance/full-time/welsh-student/who-qualifies/

Student Finance Partial Cancellation Scheme – https://www.studentfinancewales.co.uk/undergradu ate-finance/full-time/welsh-student/repaying-student-finance/

Open University access courses – https://www.open.ac.uk/courses/do-it/access

Open University list of eligible courses for Student Finance Wales funding for students who already have undergraduate degrees – https://www.open.ac.uk/courses/fees-and-funding/equivalent-qualifications

National Minimum Wage rates – https://www.gov.uk/national-minimum-wage-rates

Higher Education Funding Council for Wales (HEFCW) – https://www.hefcw.ac.uk/en/

Commission for Tertiary Education and Research in Wales (CETR) – https://www.gov.wales/tertiary-education-and-research-commission

Reaching Wider initiative (including Live Local, Learn Local community courses) – https://reachingwider.ac.uk/

Well-being of Future Generations (Wales) Act 2015 – https://www.futuregenerations.wales/about-us/future-generations-act/

A NEW ERA FOR THE ARTS IN WALES: WHAT IS IT WE WANT?

By Yvonne Murphy

An urban myth was doing the rounds nearly ten years ago on social media. It went something like this: 'When Winston Churchill was asked to cut arts funding in favour of the war effort, he simply replied, "then what are we fighting for?"' There is no known record of Churchill actually saying this. He did say: 'The arts are essential to any complete national life. The State owes it to itself to sustain and encourage them.'

A Second World War provided a horrific impetus for us to imagine the society we wanted post war, leading to the creation of the NHS and the Arts Council. Over seventy years later we must once again seriously consider what kind of society we want and think about not why, but how, the creative sector and creatives and artists are part of that reimagining. We need some fresh radical thinking and to enable that we must ensure creatives and artists are 'at the table' and embed them in our decision making processes.

In the recent Arts Council of Wales investment review in the autumn of 2023, 139 organisation across Wales, and across all art forms, applied for the holy grail of multi-year funding. 81 organisations were successful, 23 of which were awarded core funding for the first time. Of the 58 who didn't make the grade a handful were previously core funded, the largest of those being National

Theatre of Wales.[1] This process follows hot on the heels of Arts Council England's investment review which also oversaw large scale organisations losing their funding and was also followed by much analysis and challenge of the process and decision-making. The recurring theme is that arts councils are making tough decisions with too small a pot of gold and whatever way they slice the pie there's not going to be enough to go around.

There are so many questions which need answers. Questions concerning the process of an investment review where micro organisations, led by one or two freelance creatives without core funding, are asked to go through the same process and are judged by the same standards as large scale core funded and well-resourced organisations with salaried members of staff. Questions around why a review of English language theatre in Wales, or theatre as a whole, was not conducted prior to the investment review and why strategies for all art forms were not already in place before these sector changing decisions were made. (All companies who applied had to have their house in order with all policies and business plans and strategies in place – which begs the question of why Arts Council of Wales did not also have to do the same?).

Questions about how the separation of art forms within live performance impacts both artists and audiences, and what the role of any national arts organisation is within the wider ecology, and how an investment review affects

---

[1] 'National Theatre Wales Funding Axed', *Wales Arts Review*. September 27th, 2023. https://www.walesartsreview.org/national-theatre-wales-funding-axed/

that whole ecology including freelancers. Then there are also ongoing questions around transparency and accountability and boards and leadership and pay and a salaried versus a freelance workforce. For example, why is there no public pay scale for the sector? Why do some leaders earn 70-90k a year whilst many in the sector struggle to make ends meet and push above the mid 20k range? Why were micro organisations applying for the first time told that their asks, and proposed salaries above 40k for the leaders of those organisations, were considered too high when no official pay scale exists? And does a leader of a large scale organisation really deserve a higher salary than a micro organisation (or a freelancer) when it could be argued that the workload and responsibility of everything – from strategy to operations and finance, fundraising and marketing and the writing of every single piece of copy and policy – falls onto the shoulder of one, or possibly two, individuals?

But, this essay is concerned with a wider lens – and one question: How should the state 'sustain and encourage the arts' going forward if we agree that they are 'essential to any complete national life'?

Let's begin with that phrase, 'the arts', and take a step back in history before we look to the future.

The foundation of the Arts Councils that we know today was laid in 1940 when a Committee for Encouragement of Music and the Arts (CEMA) was set up during the war: 'to carry music, drama and pictures to places which otherwise would be cut off from all contact with the masterpieces of happier days and times: to air-raid shelters, to war-time hostels, to factories, to mining villages [...] the duty of C.E.M.A. was to maintain the opportunities of artistic performance for the hard-pressed and often exiled civilians,' wrote John Maynard Keynes.[2] C.E.M.A's initial aim was to 'replace what had been taken away' by war, but 'we soon found that we were providing what had never existed even in peace time.'

This led to The Arts Council of Britain being founded in 1946. The shift away from 'the arts' being seen as a private good, a luxury affordable to only a minority, to a public good accessible and available to all, had begun in earnest. However C.E.M.A's, and in turn the arts council's, vision and objective of supporting and 'spreading' what many termed 'elite culture' or 'high art' created tensions and sparked criticisms which continue to reverberate to this very day – despite the significant change of direction and scope with the appointment of Jenny Lee as the first Arts Minister in 1964.

The subsequent period from the appointment of Lee to the beginning of the Thatcher premiership is often regarded as the 'golden age' of the Arts Council, with increased access to artistic practice, support for avant-garde art forms and 'a redefinition of popular culture away from reductive assignations to the commercial sphere.[3]' State funded arts thrived for over a decade, including

---

[2] 'The Arts Council of Britain 1st Annual Report 1945' https://www.artscouncil.org.uk/sites/default/files/download-file/The%20Arts%20Council%20of%20Great%20Britain%20-%201st%20Annual%20Report%201945_0.pdf.

[3] 'Cultural Battles: Margaret Thatcher, the Greater London Council and the British Community Arts Movement', Open Edition Journals, XXVI-3. 2021. https://journals.openedition.org/rfcb/8435.

community arts and theatre-in-education, reaching a high point in the late seventies. However, with a political backlash to Keynian economics at the end of the seventies, and the prioritisation of a market-led economy, came a backlash to the very principles and vision which had formed the arts council. The principle of state-sponsored cultural production and cultural democracy were challenged, and a new cultural strategy of reduced public expenditure and the growth of private sponsorship, philanthropy and commercial imperatives began.

The notion of arts and culture being a private good gained new ground and a three pillar funding model for the arts was established – state, philanthropy, commercial – which has remained mainly unchallenged ever since, as I discussed in a blog back in 2015.[4] Those commercial imperatives meant that the 'creative industries' were separated out from arts and culture and heritage and treated as entirely separate because they could be monetised, and were therefore apparently worth a different level of investment, without any seeming understanding that the creative sector is one ecology.

A performer, a writer, a designer, a director will move across art forms and creative genres from screen, to gaming, to animation and then across all aspects of live performance because it is one ecology. A visual artist will work with a recording artist, a spoken-word poet, a musician, a tightrope walker, a games designer and a film

---

[4] 'Why fundraising & crowdfunding are not the answer Mr Skates', Omidaze Productions, Yvonne's Blog. January 21st, 2015. https://omidaze.wordpress.com /2015/01/21/why-fundraising-crowdfunding-is-not-the-answer-mr-skates/

director and see no boundaries. As a freelancer I create work with and for theatres, venues, art galleries, museums, schools, colleges, film and theatre festivals and across multi-media platforms. I work in both participatory and community arts settings as well as with 'high art' organisations and across the creative industries. Because it is one creative sector. Within this ecology I also include publications like *Wales Arts Review* where this essay was first published which are a vital component of a healthy creative sector, providing a critical lens, a platform for creative voices and public access to the work.

A starting point therefore would be to accept and acknowledge that we have one creative sector and move on from the pre-war term 'arts' and the more recent term 'culture', both of which alienate and segregate. Instead of unhelpful and artificial categories imposed on us – 'the creative industries', 'the arts', 'the arts and cultural sector', 'visual and performing arts' – could we begin to use one term to describe one ecology inside which all artists and creatives exist? The term the Creative Sector would perhaps suffice?

A second stage would be to address the unhelpful requirement for the sector to constantly articulate and defend its very existence. Creatives have been in a position of defence in the UK for decades, since Margaret Thatcher came to power and called for the arts and cultural sector to make the case for culture and define it in economic terms. Over forty years later we are still required to constantly re-articulate and re-evidence the value and impact of arts, culture and creativity to society, and spend scarce resources having to explain and defend what every individual knows is fundamental to being human. The creative sector has become increasingly mired in evidence gathering and data collection to prove its worth and very existence to society.

There is endless qualitative and quantitative evidence of the impact that access to, and participation in, creative arts and cultural activities has on everything from mental health and well-being to tackling anti-social behaviour and polarisation and increasing civic engagement and cohesive communities. The evidence also points to the benefits of using the arts and creativity in rehabilitation, conflict resolution, team building, as a diplomatic tool and 'soft power'[5] and as the most effective and low-cost strategy for urban regeneration, to name just a few areas.

If we accept all of the above we can move on from the 'why' to the 'how' and begin to look at how we fund that one ecology, that one creative sector.

The vision of one organisation to fund that one ecology which was arms-length from the government was a strong and clear vision. Unfortunately the notion of creatives being funded at arms-length has been recently undermined by Westminster through the levelling up funding which leapfrogged devolved parliaments and arts councils. It has also been somewhat undermined in Wales by the creation of Creative Wales, which is a government run agency, which has also further cemented the false

---

[5] 'Global Britain: the UK's soft power advantage', British Council. July 2021. https://www.britishcouncil.org/research-insight/global-britain-uk-soft-power-advantage-report.

divide between the 'creative industries' and 'the arts and cultural sector'.

Whilst I applaud Creative Wales for creating a long overdue memorandum of understanding with the Arts Council of Wales, it still does not answer the question of why we need two separate organisations. Particularly in a small nation where we need less structures and bureaucracy and more collaboration, partnership working and joined up thinking if we are to meet the goals and ways of working set out in the Well-being of Future Generations Act. If we accept we have one ecology, one creative sector, then surely we need one independent arms-length constitution free from red tape to invest in that sector, and with enough money to do so properly?

If we accept the return on investment into the creative sector, and that it is the fastest growing[6] sector in the UK economy, it would seem to be a no-brainer to invest in that winning horse.

The Arts Council of Wales in the most recent investment review had applications to the total of almost £54 million submitted to them. This is a good indicator of how much is required. The funding available to the Arts Council of Wales at the time of the Investment Review, to spend on core funding for arts organisations across the whole of Wales, was less than 30 million. This included cutting their own overheads to increase the spend from the previous £28.7 million.

---

[6] 'UK's Creative Industries contributes almost £13 million to the UK economy every hour', www.gov.uk. February 6th, 2020. https://www.gov.uk/government/news/uks-creative-industries-contributes-almost-13-million-to-the-uk-economy-every-hour.

To put this in context, the Welsh Government had an annual budget of £21 billion.[7] At the time, the Arts Council received £33.3 million[8] in 2023/24, a 1.5% decrease from the previous year. That amounts to 0.15% of the overall budget. To give further context, the average government spend on culture in European countries is 1%,[9] with some reaching 2.5%. The UK and Wales is shockingly below this average and yet as a sector we consistently punch above our weight on the global stage. And yet rather than this percentage being increased since this article was originally published Arts Council Wales (ACW) are now facing a further cut of 10.5% on their budget for 2024/25 from the Welsh Government. As a result ACW have had to review all costs, including being forced to make a 2.5% cut to all initial offers made to 81 successful Investment Review organisations. Taking into account all devolved nation governments being faced with difficult decisions due to standstill devolution settlements from the UK Government, questions must still be asked about the Welsh Government's lack of priority being given to the fastest growing sector in the UK economy. Such low investment is simply not

---

[7] 'Welsh Government's Budget 2022-23 - Chair's Blog', Senedd Cymru. February 2nd 2022. https://senedd.wales/senedd-now/senedd-blog/welsh-government-s-budget-2022-23-chair-s-blog/.

[8] 'Welsh Government cuts funding to Arts Council Wales', Arts Professional. December 15th 2022. https://www.artsprofessional.co.uk/news/newsreel/welsh-government-cuts-funding-arts-council-wales.

[9] 'Government expenditure on cultural, broadcasting and publishing services', Eurostat Statistics Explained. February 29th, 2024. https://ec.europa.eu/eurostat/statistics-explained/index.php?title=Culture_statistics_-_government_expenditure_on_cultural,_broadcasting_and_publishing_services&oldid=554580#:~:text=In%202021%2C%20general%20governmen t%20expenditure,of%20all%20general%20government%20expenditure.

justifiable. Rather than backing the winning horse we are neglecting and under-nourishing it to a fatal degree.

If we can own our own narrative and terminology then the question would change to – 'How do we sustain and encourage the creative sector going forward?'

To summarise, my answer to this question is in five parts:

1 We first need to accept that the creative sector is the third pillar of our civilised society, as forged post World War II. Those three pillars are a state funded NHS to nurture our health, state funded education to nurture the minds of the next generation and a state funded creative sector to nurture our souls, our spirit and give us a means to both express and understand ourselves and each other.

2 We need to acknowledge and accept that the creative sector more than 'washes its face' when it comes to the economy, as was evidenced once again with recently released figures from the Department for Culture, Media and Sport.[10]

3 We need to move from the 'why' to the 'how', and acknowledge and accept the sector's huge worth, value and benefit to society, beyond economical – and stop asking artists to prove over and over again how they can impact and benefit society.

---

[10] 'Performing arts among fastest growing sectors of economy', artsprofessional.co.uk. September 28th, 2023. https://www.arts professional.co.uk/news/performing-arts-among-fastest-growing-sectors-economy#:~:text=Data%20in%20the%20DCMS%2.

4 As a sector, let's start calling ourselves one thing. Let's own the language and the narrative. Let's call ourselves the Creative Sector. Let's accept and celebrate all the variation of creativity that exists within our sector and acknowledge that we work within one ecology that requires all of its parts to exist and thrive.

5 Then together as once unstoppable force let's begin to collectively demand a simpler state funding system and a minimum of 1% of the annual budget that can actually sustain and encourage that creative sector to flourish and thrive within the UK and on the global stage.

DEVOLUTIONARY

Manon Steffan Ros

Recently, I visited Cardiff. I stayed in one of the statuesque but soulless hotels in the bay, all magnolia walls and mood lighting. After a day's work, I ventured out into the soft, flattering sheen of light pollution by the water, and passed through the scents that spilled through the doors of restaurants, watched the skaters and felt the deep satisfying white noise of their wheels on the concrete. I read, for the hundredth time, the writing on the wall at the Millenium Centre – *Creu gwir fel gwydr o ffwrnais awen,* the words of Gwyneth Lewis, and her presence, too, always there in Wales's most quirky and brave building. I allowed myself to feel like part of the city.

The Senedd rose before me, all glass and slate. I knew the exact hue of that slate, the feel of it under my hands – I'd been to Cwt y Bugail in Llan Ffestiniog where it was quarried, had seen the gouged-out scars it had left in the mountain. The glass reflected the night back to me, as if there was nothing at all beyond it, just an empty void. And I wondered where the fourteen-year-old Manon had gone, and wherever she was, should she be occupying some small space within that building?

They used to call me a ball-breaker, back when I was fourteen – a label that I was quite proud of back then, and am horrified by today, looking back at photos of that child who was far more naive than she cared to admit. In 1997, I wore camo-print tops and a fake fur coat in a misguided attempt to look as cool as Scary Spice. I dyed my hair blue and wore huge plastic rings on my fingers, and carried permanent markers with me in order to write Oscar Wilde quotations on the walls of public toilets. I loved Lambert and Butler Menthols and Skunk Anansie and deliberately chipped nail varnish.

I was also obsessed with politics.

I wore a Labour Party badge on my school tie, and could tell you the name and constituency of the cabinet, shadow cabinet, and all Welsh MPs and a whole lot of the English ones too. I went to Labour meetings and happily joined committees, studied policy documents and could be relied upon to bore anyone at any given time. Somewhere, please God no-one look for it, but somewhere there is footage of me giving a heartfelt speech at the Welsh conference, like a cooler lefty proto-William Hague. I was so certain that politics was going to be my life's work, and everyone around me believed it too.

I wasn't going to be an MP. I was going to be an MS.

Wales *would* have its own government, and I was going to help it happen. I campaigned tirelessly for devolution. I knocked on doors, distributed leaflets, and was told to fuck off hundreds of times. Someone set their snarling German Shepherd at me.

I was part of the phone bank, where phones were slammed down more often than not. One person started a furious, lengthy tirade about Welsh separatist extremism, dotted with the most offensive and heartfelt swearwords, when I realised that I was, in fact, speaking to the father of one of my schoolfriends. "Mr—?" I said, when he paused to take a breath. "It's Manon." There was a pause, before he put the phone down, never to look me in the eye again.

I had the honour (and I say that sincerely, still) of being in charge of the loudspeaker on the car which crawled the streets of Bangor in the days before the referendum on devolution. I particularly remember the day before – a Wednesday, a schoolday, so it must have been after school. I was buzzing. The referendum the next day was going to change the world, or my world, at least. Wales would govern itself with grace and elegance, proving to the rest of the world that politics can be kind, generous and fair. I had faith.

The script I had prepared for that day was simple and straightforward, and I must have repeated it hundreds of times as I was driven around Bangor by an elderly, gentle chain-smoking man whose name I have sadly forgotten. *Vote Yes for Wales tomorrow. Pleidleisiwch Ie dros Gymru yfory. Remember to turn up to use your vote. Cofiwch droi fyny i ddefnyddio eich pleidlais.* It wasn't clever or catchy or even that interesting, but each word, each syllable and inflection is imprinted in my memory. The weather was kind, and people were in their gardens, enjoying a gentle Indian summer, chatting with neighbours over their fences or having a cuppa in the sun. We must have annoyed them, a whiny, preachy version of an ice-cream van without any treats and not even a pretty, clunky song to give. They saluted us with two fingers, even the children. I vividly remember a boy, who couldn't have been that much younger than myself, raced in front of the car and pulled down his trousers, bent over and showing us his bare arse. I was horrified, until the chain-smoking driver beside me started cackling with mirth through his cigarette. I giggled too, then laughed, and we carried on.

I thought about all of this as I stood before the Senedd in Cardiff, remembering the laughter and the swearing and that moment in 1997 when I'd been so sure that were we to have devolution, all would be well. That as a young woman, there would be space for me in an assembly or senedd or whatever it might be.

I thought that my opinion mattered.

And therein lies the undeniable, unsavoury truth. Somewhere along the line, something changed. A part of it must have been a change within me, as we do all grow ever further from our great young selves. But a part of it is the climate of politics, too, and the general loss of faith in the political system. Ennui is endemic. No-one feels as though they have any measure of power over governance. In short, I have become the opposite of what I was in 1997 – I am apathetic.

***

Part of the attraction of devolution was, to me, all about words. My words, and my mother's words, and the words I spoke with my friends and teachers and boyfriends and enemies. Having been raised on a diet of protests by Cymdeithas yr Iaith Gymraeg, with family friends regularly disappearing for spells in jail for their political activism, I cannot remember a time when I felt that my mother tongue wasn't under attack. I can't begin to unpick the psychological impact of growing up feeling that the very words in one's mouth were hated by some, dismissed as irrelevant by many more. To me, and to so many others, there was a constant underlying awareness that some people were offended by the language of our mothers' lullabies, or the words our teachers used to engage and enrage us, or the words our dolls spoke to one another.

How can you *not* be political when your tool of communication is so often a punchline?

A rant about the bias against the Welsh language might seem like a red herring here, but many of us hoped that having a measure of self-governance for Wales would legitimise our language in a political landscape that seemed to ignore its very existence. Has it been a success? Oddly enough, I don't feel qualified to answer that question. The Senedd was built and First Ministers have come and gone, and I am in my forties now, and have changed alongside the political landscape. I believe that more of an effort is made to preserve and protect the Welsh language from the Senedd than has been done from Westminster, but, to be embarrassingly anecdotal about it: not many speak Welsh on the streets anymore despite the efforts of the Senedd. We need to do better.

This is all predictably personal, of course, and for that I make no apology. Everyone has a burning issue that becomes their own yardstick for measuring a government's success. Do the trains run on time? What's the unemployment rate? For me, I will always hope for a government that is naturally, effortlessly bilingual, and for that to be a part of governance, not tied to whoever happens to be running the show at any particular time. I would like for the use of my language not to be a political statement.

***

I am proud of that 1997 Manon. I admire her tenacity, her faith in her own opinion and voice. And I am proud that I was a small part of a sea change in Wales. The Senedd has its problems, and its potential is far from being realised – but let's not make the easy mistake of confusing the institution with the people who are running it. The elected Members of the Senedd are overwhelmingly white, overwhelmingly middle class, overwhelmingly and boringly similar to one another. Recent reports of a culture of bullying within the Senedd are disturbing. But these failures exist because of the government we have elected to run the institution, not because of the institution itself. The difference in the public perception of the Senedd versus the Houses of Parliament is stark here. An unpopular policy directed from Westminster will launch a tirade of complaints about the Tories or Labour, but no-one calls for the abolition of the Commons. But change the speed limit on some roads in Wales, and people will vehemently demand that the Senedd should cease to exist. Trust reverts to the UK government, and the lack of self-belief behind that saddens me.

If you would have told me twenty-five years ago that I'd no longer even know the name of the Welsh leader of the Liberal Democrats, or which constituency the culture minister represents, or that I was no longer a member of any political party and have no affinity with them either, I would have been disgusted with myself. I was going to occupy that space in Cardiff Bay, and I was going to be the person beyond the reflection of the people who gaze into the Senedd building, eyes glittering, wondering whilst wandering. I would be part of a revolution of kindness, ensuring politics was open and caring and responsible.

But the Senedd, like Westminster, is none of those things. Politicians are routinely bullied online, threatened with violence, made to feel unsafe. Women, in particular, are attacked with the venom of age-old misogyny, as if any measure of power is somehow unfeminine. There's a special and terrible poison reserved for young women who are powerful, straightforward orators – and, without blowing my trumpet, that's who I would have been.

Had I followed my planned trajectory into politics, I have no doubt in my mind that I would now be living in fear. People would hate the fact that I have a loud voice and louder opinions. My career would serve as proof that I wasn't a good or present mother to my children. People would tweet about my spare tyre showing under my jacket, and that my hair was badly dyed, and that I needed a stylist because who in their right mind would wear lipstick that bright every day. Frankly, any woman who is willing to put herself through that for the greater good has my respect, and my bafflement too.

I am envious of their faith that they have the power to change things.

On my visit to Cardiff, I felt curiously proud of that huge, reflective building, imposing but somehow dignified. It's not a place that feels as if it belongs to me, but perhaps that doesn't matter – perhaps the energy and vivaciousness of my young self is right there, between those Llan Ffestiniog slates or blurred in the reflections of the sky and the sea. When I search hard for it, I find hope within myself for the Senedd, and for devolution, for I trust the younger generation far more than I trust my own. We can be great. We can create a system that isn't based on a model from another place, from another time. I am so glad that devolution happened, but we have to be brave about it, and creative too. Perhaps we're in the wrong building. The nearby Millenium Centre, with Gwyneth Lewis's words emblazoned across it, might serve as a good motto for devolution – *Creu gwir fel gwydr o ffwrnais awen*. The latter, lovely Cymraeg literally translates as *Creating truth like glass from the furnace of inspiration*.

BIOGRAPHICAL NOTES ON CONTRIBUTORS

Sophie Buchaillard

Sophie Buchaillard's novel *Assimilation* (Honno) explores identity and migration. Her debut novel *This is Not Who We Are* (Seren) was shortlisted for the Wales Book of the Year 2023. In 2016, Sophie co-authored *Talented Women for a Successful Wales*, a report advising the Welsh Government on improving gender parity in education and business. She served on the Welsh Government's Women in STEM Board as an independent advisor and was shortlisted for a Womenspire Award in 2017 for this work. Sophie holds a PhD in Creative and Critical Writing from Cardiff University.

X/Instagram: @growriter

Michelle Deininger

Dr Michelle Deininger is Interim Director of Lifelong Learning at Cardiff University and Senior Lecturer in Humanities. She teaches a range of courses in Literature, Creative Writing, and Cultural Studies, aimed at adult learners and often involving the end of the world. Her writing and research is focused on environmental humanities, Welsh women writers, and the idea of apocalypse. She is especially interested in class and education and has written and spoken on this topic in various contexts.

Jasmine Donahaye

Jasmine Donahaye is the author of six books, including *Birdsplaining: A Natural History* (2023), *Losing Israel* (2015) and *The Greatest Need* (2015). Her work has appeared in the *Guardian* and the *New York Times*, and on Radio 4. She is a Professor of Creative Writing at Swansea University, and is a Fellow of the Learned Society of Wales.

Mari Ellis Dunning

Mari Ellis Dunning's debut poetry collection, *Salacia*, was shortlisted for Wales Book of the Year 2019. She has since placed second in both the Lucent Dreaming Short Story Competition and the Sylvia Plath Poetry Prize. Mari is a PhD candidate at Aberystwyth University, where she is using creative practice to explore the relationship between accusations of witchcraft in Wales and the reproductive body. Her poetry collection *Pearl and Bone* was selected as *Wales Arts Review*'s Number 1 of 2022, and is available from Parthian. Mari lives on the west coast of Wales with her husband, their two sons, and their very adorable poochon. She is the founder of Pay for Poets, a free resource to help writers earn a living through their work.

Nansi Eccott

Nansi Eccott is a future trainee solicitor and current Legal Practice Course student at Cardiff University. Whilst studying an undergraduate degree in Law and Welsh at Cardiff, Nansi was fortunate to undertake a policy placement with WEN Wales.

Rae Howells

Rae Howells is a poet, journalist, academic and lavender farmer. Her debut collection, *The language of bees* (Parthian), was shortlisted for the Wales Book of the Year 2023. She has previously won both the Rialto Nature and Place, and Welsh International, poetry competitions and featured in journals including *Magma*, *The Rialto*, *Poetry Wales*, *New Welsh Review*, *Acumen* and *Poetry Ireland*. A former hyperlocal journalist, she studied the death of local newspapers for her PhD, and co-authored *Hyperlocal Journalism* (Routledge, 2018). Rae's new poetry collection, *This Common Uncommon*, is a response to a hyperlocal nature emergency in her neighbourhood, and is forthcoming with Parthian in 2024. Read more at raehowells.co.uk, and find out more about her business, Gower Lavender, at gowerlavender.co.uk

Jessica Laimann

Jessica Laimann is the Policy and Public Affairs Manager at the Women's Equality Network (WEN) Wales, where she leads on policy, research and advocacy work. She has experience in devolved and local government and a research background in feminist theory and philosophy.

Krystal S. Lowe

Krystal S. Lowe is a Bermuda-born, Wales-based dancer, choreographer, writer, and director performing and creating dance theatre works for stage, public space, and film that explore themes of intersectional identity, mental health and wellbeing, and empowerment to challenge herself and audiences toward introspection and social change. She's passionate about integrating access and exploring multilingual work with a specific focus on British Sign Language, Welsh, and English.

Currently, she is Associate Artist for Ballet Cymru, Trustee for National Dance Company Wales, and 2023 Arts Foundation Fellow finalist for Dance Theatre.

Cerith Mathias

Cerith Mathias is a journalist, producer, and festival director. She is Contributing Editor of *Wales Arts Review* and writes on arts and culture for publications in the UK and US, with a particular interest in literature from the Deep South. A journalist and producer with BBC Wales for almost 20 years, Cerith was at the helm of political, current affairs and large-scale live TV programmes. Now a freelance journalist, she continues to produce programmes for BBC Wales, ITV Wales and S4C. She's a founding director of Cardiff Book Festival and Pontypridd Children's Book Festival and co-owner of Storyville Books, the only independent bookshop in the South Wales Valleys. She is a member of Monumental Welsh Women, the group behind the Hidden Heroines campaign which resulted in the unveiling of The Betty Campbell Monument in Cardiff, the Elaine Morgan statue in Mountain Ash and the Cranogwen statue in Llangrannog.

Yvonne Murphy

Yvonne Murphy is a freelance theatre director and producer who runs Omidaze Productions and is the creator of The Democracy Box and The Talking Shop. Yvonne works widely across both the creative and democracy sectors and is particularly interested in the intersection between Cultural and Democratic Participation, Access and Engagement, Alternative Economic and Business Models and Creative Learning.

Grace Quantock

Grace Quantock is a cross-disciplinary academic and activist researcher in psychotherapy and counselling, emerging digital technologies and inclusion. She graduated from the School of Education at Bath Spa University with a Masters in 2021 and is a guest lecturer at the University of South Wales, supporting the Children and Adolescent Mental Health MA.

In addition, Grace has research experience in psychotherapy and emerging technologies and has undertaken AHRC-funded research fellowships with UWE Bristol, in partnership with Watershed, Bristol, Kaleider in Exeter and Bath Spa University, the University of Plymouth and Falmouth University. Grace is also a resident of the Pervasive Media Studio, Watershed, Bristol.

Manon Steffan Ros

Manon Steffan Ros is a novelist, playwright, games author, scriptwriter and musician. She is the author of over twenty children's books and three novels for adults, all in Welsh. She has won the Wales Book of the Year as well as being four-times winner of the Tir na N'Og Welsh children's literature award. She has also won Eisteddfod and National Theatre Wales awards for her drama writing. She lives in north Wales with her two sons and daughter. In 2023 she won the Yoto Carnegie Medal for *The Blue Book of Nebo*, her English translation of her novel Llyfr Glas Nebo. It was the first novel in translation to win in the eighty-seven year history of the award. It has since been translated into many languages.

Norena Shopland

Norena Shopland has a Master's degree in heritage studies and has worked for the British Museum, National Museums Scotland and the Museum of London among others. Now living back in Wales she has worked with leading heritage organisations including National Museums Wales, Glamorgan Archives and Cardiff Story Museum.

Shopland has extensively researched the heritage of LGBT people and issues in Wales for 15 years. She devised the first project in Wales to look at placing sexual orientation and gender identity into Welsh history, culminating in the Welsh Pride, the first exhibition exclusively on Welsh LGBT people, allies and events, and managed Gender Fluidity, the first funded transgender project in Wales. She arranged for Gillian Clarke to write the first poem in the world by a national or poet laureate celebrating the LGBT people of a country. Her work has appeared in the Welsh press, radio and TV and she regularly provides advice and support on the history of LGBT people in Wales. She lectures to staff networks from the Welsh Government, to numerous museums, archives, charities and other events such as BiFest, Sparkle, Aberration.

PARTHIAN

WALES: ENGLAND'S COLONY?

Martin Johnes

From the very beginnings of Wales, its people have defined themselves against their large neighbour. This book tells the fascinating story of an uneasy and unequal relationship between two nations living side-by-side.

PB / £8.99
978-1-912681-41-9

RHYS DAVIES: A WRITER'S LIFE

Meic Stephens

Rhys Davies (1901-78) was among the most dedicated, prolific and accomplished of Welsh prose writers. This is his first full biography.

'This is a delightful book, which is itself a social history in its own right, and funny.'
– The Spectator

PB / £11.99
978-1-912109-96-8

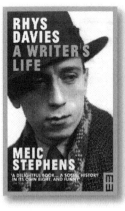

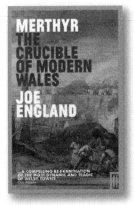

MERTHYR, THE CRUCIBLE OF MODERN WALES

Joe England

Merthyr Tydfil was the town where the future of a country was forged: a thriving, struggling surge of people, industry, democracy and ideas. This book assesses an epic history of Merthyr from 1760 to 1912 through the focus of a fresh and thoroughly convincing perspective.

PB / £18.99
978-1-913640-05-7

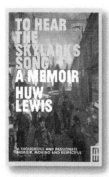

TO HEAR THE SKYLARK'S SONG

Huw Lewis

To Hear the Skylark's Song is a memoir about how Aberfan survived and eventually thrived after the terrible disaster of the 21st of October 1966.

'A thoughtful and passionate memoir, moving and respectful.'
– Tessa Hadley

PB / £8.99
978-1-912109-72-2

ROCKING THE BOAT

Angela V. John

This insightful and revealing collection of essays focuses on seven Welsh women who, in a range of imaginative ways, resisted the status quo in Wales, England and beyond during the nineteenth and twentieth centuries.

PB / £11.99
978-1-912681-44-0

TURNING THE TIDE

Angela V. John

This rich biography tells the remarkable tale of Margaret Haig Thomas (1883-1958) who became the second Viscountess Rhondda. She was a Welsh suffragette, held important posts during the First World War and survived the sinking of the *Lusitania*.

PB / £17.99
978-1-909844-72-8

BRENDA CHAMBERLAIN, ARTIST & WRITER

Jill Piercy

The first full-length biography of Brenda Chamberlain chronicles the life of an artist and writer whose work was strongly affected by the places she lived, most famously Bardsey Island and the Greek island of Hydra.

PB / £11.99
978-1-912681-06-8

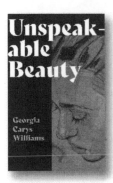

UNSPEAKABLE BEAUTY
Georgia Carys Williams

This beautiful, poetic debut novel warns of the dangers of being a quiet person in a loud world and letting magnetic strangers pull your strings. Set on the Welsh coast, it is an unsettling coming-of-age tale about the importance of learning how to take the lead and be yourself, of finding hope in the shadows, of letting your dreams bloom.

PB / £10.99
978-1-914595-42-4

THE HALF-LIFE OF SNAILS
Philippa Holloway

LONGLISTED FOR THE RSL ONDAATJE PRIZE 2023

'A powerful, evocative novel about landscape, about a young mother living near a nuclear power plant in Wales... I thought it was a terrific book.' – Samira Ahmed, *Front Row*, BBC Radio 4

PB / £9.99
978-1-914595-52-3

EASY MEAT
Rachel Trezise

'A sensitive portrayal of people as people – full, complex and multifaceted – whose every choice is shaped by the conflicting experiences and identities that inform who we are.'
– Polly Winn, *the Welsh Agenda*

'A one-sitting page-turner that gives voice to the voiceless while checking the country's pulse' – Dylan Moore

PB / £10.00
978-1-914595-87-5

PIGEON
Alys Conran

WINNER OF WALES BOOK OF THE YEAR / SHORTLISTED FOR THE DYLAN THOMAS PRIZE

'An exquisite novel by a great new talent.' – M.J. Hyland

'...might have been authored by Faulkner... pitch-perfect.'
– Omar Sabbagh, New Welsh Review

PB / £9.99
978-1-910901-23-6